Condensed Milk

Conversations with God

Condensed Milk

Conversations with God

J. David Cummings

Condensed Milk

By J. David Cummings

www.condensedmilkbook.com

© 2014 J. David Cummings

All rights reserved. No portion of this book may be reproduced, stored in a retrieval system, or transmitted in any form or by any means - electronic, mechanical, photocopy, recording, scanning, or any other - except for brief quotations in critical reviews or articles, without the prior written permission of the publisher.

Scripture quotations taken from the New American Standard Bible®, Copyright © 1960, 1962, 1963, 1968, 1971, 1972, 1973, 1975, 1977, 1995 by The Lockman Foundation. Used by permission. (www.Lockman.org)

ISBN-10: 0-9912491-0-0

ISBN-13: 978-0-9912491-0-7

Printed in U.S.A.

First Edition Printing 2014

Cover Design by Trenton League

http://leaguedesigns.com/

Reader's comments

Condensed Milk

I love this book! I just want to sit around and share God stories with you. This book makes you hungry for more of Him! It opens hearts up to possibilities of more encounters with the Lord! Nothing is better than that!

-Kim Deal, Follower of Jesus

David, I LOL when I read the title. That's beautiful. I want you to know that I know it is much more than condensed milk. There is a meat offering also to the discerning. It is a marvelous table wine from the heavenly vineyards, a sweet smelling savor from and unto the Lord and His body.

-Joel Montgomery, Man of God and Mentor

The title, *Condensed Milk,* refers to Paul's statement:

> *I gave you milk to drink, not solid food; for you were not yet able to receive it. Indeed, even now you are not yet able,*
>
> 1 Corinthians 3:2

The Lord had told me He would give me a good title for this book. I kept coming up with titles that were good but there were plenty of other books written with those titles. I was praying about the book and He referred to it as "milk" and said, "condensed milk." I liked the title but argued that I thought there was plenty of meat in here too. I thought we should call it *Condensed Milk with Meat Sauce.* He didn't respond. Nobody else liked the meat sauce idea either.

Contents

Foreword .... - 9 -
Preface .... - 11 -
1. This Changes Everything .... - 13 -
2. You Left Your Lights On .... - 21 -
3. Forgiveness .... - 25 -
4. Driving a Car off a Cliff .... - 33 -
5. The Big Greenhouse .... - 37 -
6. The Prayer of a 12-Year-Old .... - 43 -
7. The Church .... - 45 -
8. Speaking in Tongues .... - 49 -
9. Runaway Love .... - 59 -
10. Praying for the Nations .... - 63 -
11. Sticking Pennies to the Wall .... - 67 -
12. Trusting God .... - 73 -
13. I Come Quickly .... - 79 -
14. The Trinity .... - 85 -
15. Falling Out in the Spirit .... - 87 -
16. Laying on of Hands .... - 93 -
17. Resist Evil, Even Unto Death .... - 97 -
18. The Daisy Bucket Anointing .... - 101 -
19. Revival, Laughter .... - 105 -
20. The Halloween Bible .... - 109 -
21. The Seven Tests of Man .... - 111 -

22. Fear of Man	- 115 -
23. The Fear of the Lord	- 121 -
24. You Can't Out Give God	- 135 -
25. The Wilderness	- 143 -
26. Rome Wasn't Built in a Day	- 145 -
27. Conversations with God	- 151 -
28. Little Helicopters	- 157 -
29. His Love	- 161 -
30. Why Worship?	- 167 -
31. God Sent Me an Email	- 171 -
32. Prophetic Dreams	- 177 -
33. Superheroes	- 181 -
34. The Mighty Power of God	- 187 -
35. Manifestations	- 191 -
36. The Dark Side	- 201 -
37. Raising from the Dead	- 205 -
38. John Chapter 17	- 207 -
39. Third Heaven	- 211 -
40. The Hound of Heaven	- 217 -
41. Stranded	- 223 -
Epilogue	- 233 -
End Notes	- 237 -

Foreword

My husband is a reluctant and unlikely author. He writes not out of desire but from his obedience to God, for the purpose of recording the many blessings and supernatural events we have experienced. I love that he writes exactly the way he talks. His style is more like a collection of "blogs."

David is far from a perfect man, and he will be the first to tell you that. What he is though is "a man after God's own heart." The many encounters he has had with God are a direct result of his desire to know Him and seek Him and spending bazillions of hours with Him during the wee hours of the morn, on the way to work and back, during his lunch break, during the night watches, on his days off, etc., seeking Him, talking to Him and listening to God.

The most important part is listening. God still speaks to man. If you listen, you will hear Him. Just as the sheep learn to recognize the voice of their shepherd, so can we.

We are big believers in sharing our testimony. The Bible says they overcame him by the blood of the Lamb and the word of their testimony (Rev 12:11). Imagine that ... our God-encounters rate right up there with Jesus' death and resurrection. That is an honor and a responsibility of the highest calling.

I can attest to the validity and accuracy of David's stories, for many of them we experienced together. They are inspiring, moving, surreal, supernatural and unbelievable. I confess that I even got goose bumps when reading some of them.

Our heart's desire is that you will be touched by God and compelled to believe that there is more to be found in this life, your relationship, encounters and conversations with Him.

Blessings to all who read this work and seek to know God and know Him more fully.

Alison Cummings

Preface

A long time ago someone prophesied that I would write a book. Then over the years as we told excerpts of our testimony people would say, "You should write that down." Then the Lord told me to write a book. He said, "If you'll just sit down at the computer, I'll give you words to write."

I'm hoping this book will find its way into the hands of serious men and women of God. My prayer and heart's desire is that this book will inspire you to press in to know Lord Jesus better, to better understand The Kingdom of God, and to make you think "outside the box," to discard any limits in your mind about what God is capable of and how committed He is to your growth.

There are things in this book you might think God wouldn't do. There are things in His book (the Bible) that are hard to believe as well. Who would have thought He would make a donkey talk (Numbers 22:28-30)?

Some of the testimonies in this book are really hard to believe, and at least one of them took me as much as four years to work through.

You are going to examine some encounters with God that may be just outside your beliefs, and if you can't get there, it's okay. You don't have to believe what I believe.

If you don't take anything else away from this I hope it will challenge you to have a deeper relationship with our Lord. To stop and just be with Him, no agenda - just hang out with Him and get to know Him. Press into Him, ask questions, listen for a response. Knowing Him, being close to Him, is better than you can imagine.

I decided years ago on a personal mission statement:

I will seek to know the Lord my God as well as a man can know his Lord and hopefully out of that relationship will flow all the ministry my heart could desire.

By the way, I am not sure if it is a result of all the time I have spent in the Word, but this book is all out of chronological order, and it's a mix of testimonies and teachings.

I hope this book is a blessing to you.

J. David Cummings

1. This Changes Everything

I start here, because this is what changed everything for me.

Most Christians believe that God heals. How He heals is up for debate. Some people believe God works only within the constraints of nature; others in miraculous, instantaneous healings. At the time, I wasn't sure if God healed at all.

Raised Southern Baptist, I'd walked the aisle to get my "fire insurance." I went to church with my family every time the doors were open until I turned 16. At that point I rebelled hard against God and left the church. After marrying Alison, God started drawing us back to Him. I'm not sure if I was a Christian or even saved at this point in my life. But my bent was toward God.

Our friends attended a Pentecostal church. They told us about a healing service their church would host occasionally on Friday nights. They encouraged us to go. I was very skeptical about healing ministries. I'd never been to a healing service or a Pentecostal church. It was outside my comfort zone. Yet, they kept telling us about these amazing healings. Their stories were fascinating. Finally we agreed to go. We wanted to see it for ourselves.

They said, "We all know you're almost blind without your glasses. If you go, let's pray and see if God will heal your eyes."

They told us it requires faith for God to heal. I purposed to believe. I decided that I would press in and trust God to heal my eyes. If He didn't, it wouldn't be because of any lack of faith on my part.

We went to the next service with our friends. There was a young minister who would point to people or call out to the congregation. He said God is healing this over here or God is doing something else over there. It appeared people were being healed all over the place. There was an elevated sense of hope, anticipation and faith in the room.

I had my eyes closed. I was standing in the balcony, praying, with my knees right up next to the rail. I didn't hear him say this - they told me afterwards - the minister pointed to the balcony in our area and said, "There's a young man receiving a healing in his leg, no, in his foot."

I didn't hear him at all because at that moment I felt a strong presence of the Lord and an intense feeling on my head. **It felt like hot oil pouring into the top of my head** and down into my body and then running through the inside of me. It was incredibly hot. It should have been painful but it wasn't. God had clearly done something. None of my muscles were working, and I wondered if I might fall over the rail. Yet something was holding me up.

My glasses were still in my pocket, so I opened my eyes. I was surprised that my vision was still impaired. I thought maybe it takes a while, so I didn't put the glasses back on - that would be a lack of faith.

As the symptoms from the hot oil treatment diminished, I was left with what felt like drunkenness. I was a very happy drunk. I couldn't really form words. Our friends just looked at me and smiled - that knowing smile.

And then the event was over. Like a herd of cattle we slowly moved to the door and left. Alison had to drive me home as I was in no condition to drive. Sometime later all the symptoms went away. As an act of faith or whatever I refused to put on my glasses all weekend.

By Sunday I was upset with God because I thought He hadn't done anything. I refused to go to church, and come Monday morning it was time for me to go back to work.

I'd had a skin disease for a long time. I don't know exactly what it was, because I couldn't afford to see a doctor.

I was missing all of the skin on three toes on my left foot and one on my right foot. That week I got a blister on my hand. You know, an unsightly skin disease is easy to hide wearing socks and shoes but the one on my hand was going to be hard to conceal.

Condensed Milk

I started my morning regimen. I had a box of over-the-counter medicine I used to treat the condition. When I lifted up my foot to start cleaning and disinfecting, I was shocked to see that I had all new skin on my foot – no scar tissue!

God even put the hairs back on my toes and the fingerprints on the bottom of my toes. In fact, the only trace you could see was the tan line that separated the new skin from the old. Incredible! Amazing! God healed my hand and both feet and the disease has not come back since.

I couldn't actually believe it, but then I couldn't deny it either. It sounds ironic now but I was finally down to believing either God healed me or the Devil did. If I could believe the Devil could heal then surely God can, as He is more powerful than the Devil. Why would the Devil do something good?

That was the way I reconciled it. I still didn't believe in miracles. In a few seconds God forced me out of my naive naturalistic world view. This was the first step - God taking my beliefs outside the box. All of a sudden I had more questions than answers. This meant God can work outside the laws of physics. Life would never be the same.

This changed everything for us. Suddenly we had stepped into the things of the Spirit, a world that we knew nothing about ...

Oh, something I failed to mention - that young minister, not well-known at the time, was Benny Hinn.[A]

Since then Alison and I have been healed many times by God and seen Him heal so many people. We've seen backs healed, a tumor disappear, a foot grow, teeth healed, teeth straightened, scars disappear, headaches go away, joints healed and the list goes on. We've heard of amazing healings that God has done all over the world. Sometimes He heals fast, sometimes He heals slow. Sometimes He heals with a doctor's help, sometimes He even heals with death.

God doesn't view death the same as we do. When we die, we are instantly with Him and are no longer suffering or incapacitated. Most of us would prefer He would not choose that method, but I doubt if the people healed by death would want to be back here after tasting heaven.

I've noticed that God is more interested in healing hearts than healing bodies. He's also very interested in relationships. Sick people are more dependent on the people around them; this builds relationships. Hardship grows us and the caregivers who love us. Sick people tend to seek God. God tends to reveal Himself in our time of need. Look at all we would miss out on if we never knew suffering.

> *to another faith by the same Spirit, and to another gifts of healing by the one Spirit,*
>
> 1 Corinthians 12:9

As Alison and I grew in our understanding of Holy Spirit's ministry of healing, we became accustomed to God's healing. It no longer required much faith. We knew God would heal like we knew it would rain. Like predicting the rain, we didn't know if God would heal instantly or not, but we were sure He would eventually.

Don't presume on God. He's a person not a method. We are His servants, not the other way around. He's God. He will do what He thinks is best for us, when He wants to. His timing is perfect.

Alison and I got the chance to go to a Healing School. Some of the most gifted ministers of healing would be there from all around the world. We were a bit embarrassed as Alison had badly torn her shoulder and I my knee. We prayed for ourselves, we prayed for each other, we asked our friends and our church ministry team to pray for us. Nada, God didn't do anything.

We went anyway. I felt like a faithless fool, limping into the class. At the end of week they let us go into the Healing Rooms as part of their ministry. People asked us what we needed prayer for, then laid hands on our injuries and prayed for God to heal us. We felt a powerful presence of the Lord. It felt like God was healing us, then nothing. We were still crippled. We went home with our injuries and they didn't get any better.

Finally we went to the doctor, then to the hospital; he operated on us and we slowly recovered. Neither of us was a hundred percent healed, even after surgery, but close enough.

What did we learn? We learned God is sovereign. We learned not to judge God when He doesn't do what we want, when we want, or how we want. We gained a lot of compassion for those who are recovering from surgery.

Funny thing, over time we discovered what God <u>did</u> do during that prayer. Alison has suffered all her adult life from terrible migraines. I have been insanely allergic to onions. We were both completely healed. Alison hasn't had a migraine since and I can eat all the onions I want in any form. Praise God, Halleluiah! These were ailments surgery couldn't fix.

He met our greatest need, not our greatest desire.

> *And my God will supply all your needs according to His riches in glory in Christ Jesus.*
>
> Philippians 4:19

Condensed Milk

2. You Left Your Lights On

Driving to work one day, I was listening to Chuck Swindoll on the radio.[B] I was surprised when he said that a person could pray while they were driving. At the time, I hadn't prayed with my eyes open before. I have a lot of time in the car going to and from work. This was a great opportunity to increase my prayer time.

The company I worked for at the time had us park in a parking garage. I usually parked on the top in the sun. As I drove through the garage I would turn my lights on because it was dark. When I reached the top in the sunlight I would occasionally not notice and leave my lights on. Often on those occasions when I left the lights on, I was also working late. When I would come out to the car - sometimes as late as 10 o'clock at night - the battery would be dead and the car wouldn't start.

Whenever this happened, I would have to call Alison for help. She would have to get our very young children out of bed, load them up in her car and drive to the office so I could jumpstart my car. Then we would all head back home and put the kids back to bed. We'd gone through this cycle several times.

One morning, as I was praying on the way to the office, I had reached the top of the parking garage, got out of the car but was not finished with my prayer. I was standing by the car looking to heaven (with my eyes open) still praying. I was talking to the Lord.

What I was trying to determine is what part of my life am I responsible for and what part of my life is He responsible for. I wanted to know what I needed to worry about and be concerned with and what He was going to be concerned with.

My expectations were fairly low. I didn't think that God cared much about the details, the little things in our life. I thought He was really only interested in the few big events in our life.

As I'm trying to determine this, the prayer kind of spun out of control. I was standing in the sunlight, looking toward heaven and at the top of my lungs, I yelled at God, **"What do you want from me?** How involved do you want to be in my life? What do you want me to be responsible for and what part of my life are you responsible for?"

I stood quietly and waited for His response.

All the Lord said calmly was, **"You left your lights on."**

I turned around to look and sure enough, I had left my lights on. He just melted my heart. I unlocked the car, turned off the lights and humbly apologized to the Lord for yelling.

I have always taken this to mean that He cares about the little things. We're important to Him, and nothing is too small for Him. And He tolerates and forgives our immaturity.

> *Are not five sparrows sold for two cents? Yet not one of them is forgotten before God. [7] Indeed, the very hairs of your head are all numbered. Do not fear; you are more valuable than many sparrows.*
>
> *Luke 12:6-7*

Before this encounter with God, I had reached an almost deistic worldview. Deists believe that God created the world then left it to operate on its own within the laws of physics.

For whatever reason I thought God would show up occasionally, keep you from being harmed, or help you make a decision now and then. But I didn't expect Him to be aware of what was going on in my life. As God continued to reveal Himself to me, my beliefs were challenged, and my theology had to change.

The truth is our God is very involved in every aspect of our lives. He knows all our concerns before we even start to pray.

> *So do not be like them; for your Father knows what you need before you ask Him.*
>
> Matthew 6:8

Even though I'd heard God speak before, this was the first time He verbally answered my prayer. His answer was carefully crafted to communicate both the truth He wanted me to know and to validate that it came from Him. His reply contained knowledge I didn't possess so I would know what He said hadn't originated in my head.

> *Do you not know? Have you not heard? The Everlasting God, the LORD, the Creator of the ends of the earth does not become weary or tired. His understanding is inscrutable.*
>
> Isaiah 40:28

I was amazed to discover that God will answer questions. This event changed my prayer life forever. I began to pray with expectation. From this point on, I would pause after each question to listen for His response.

In His loving way, He watches over and cares for us even though many are oblivious of His existence. He waits for opportunities to reveal Himself in little coincidences that still require a touch of faith. If God cares about the little things, I need to care about the little things that are important to Him. **God is love, and love always cares.**

3. Forgiveness

I was upset with someone that committed a grievous sin against me, and I asked the Lord what He was going to do and how much longer I was going to have to wait for justice.

I was surprised when the Lord told me that He had already forgiven him. I said I didn't think this guy was even a Christian.

The Lord said He died to take away the sins of the world and that His mercies are new every day.

Apparently, each day He forgives all our sins and it appears He forgives everyone's individual sins.

> *and He Himself is the propitiation for our sins; and not for ours only, but also for those of the whole world.*
>
> *1 John 2:2*

I didn't know Jesus died for the sins of the whole world. I thought He only died for those already saved. I've prayed the sinner's prayer hundreds of times. I was concerned that He hadn't forgiven my sins because I hadn't asked. Or what

Condensed Milk

if I accumulated one more sin and died without asking Him to forgive me yet? I also feared that I might do something not knowing it was sin and never ask.

My fear was based on the belief that asking for forgiveness was a requirement for salvation. It's good to pray and ask Jesus to forgive my sins but since He has forgiven me whether I ask or not it doesn't appear to be a requirement for salvation.

> *If we confess our sins, He is faithful and righteous to forgive us our sins and to cleanse us from all unrighteousness.*
>
> 1 John 1:9

The goal is not the forgiveness. Jesus paid that debt in full on the cross. The goal is overcoming sin. That process involves prayer, confession, relationship and most of all the grace we need from God.

Holy Spirit convicts us of our sin (John 16). And God leads us to repent.

> *For the sorrow that is according to the will of God produces a repentance without regret, leading to salvation, but the sorrow of the world produces death.*
>
> 2 Corinthians 7:10

Salvation

If our sins are forgiven then what must we do to be saved?

The thief on the cross didn't pray the sinner's prayer. He didn't even ask Jesus to forgive his sin. He just believed. Jesus said, "Today you'll be with me in Paradise."

> *"For God so loved the world, that He gave His only begotten Son, that whoever believes in Him shall not perish, but have eternal life.*
>
> John 3:16

Is that all we have to do, just believe? It appears so. Holy Spirit may have convicted the thief of his sins, and he may have repented. We don't know the details. The Bible doesn't say. Martin Luther emphasized that our works don't get us into heaven.[c]

> *For by grace you have been saved through faith; and that not of yourselves, it is the gift of God;* [9] *not as a result of works, so that no one may boast.*
>
> Ephesians 2:8-9

There isn't anything I can do to work my way to heaven. Good works are highly recommended for many reasons but they will not get us into heaven. All sin was paid for by Jesus.

Salvation is a free gift of God. Eternal life is so accessible and yet many will reject Jesus.

> *For the wages of sin is death, but the free gift of God is eternal life in Christ Jesus our Lord.*
>
> *Romans 6:23*

Most Christians knew little or nothing of how to be saved before they were saved. God orchestrated it all. They just knew they had an encounter with God and suddenly things were different. Salvation has been described by the phrase, "I was blind and now I see."

Some of us spend our lives searching through the natural and religious doctrines to find answers to our existential questions. Who am I? Why was I created? What is my purpose? If this describes you, I challenge you to open the Bible and turn to the book of John, pray and ask Jesus Christ to reveal himself to you. You won't be disappointed.

He is a real God, a living God, and though you've heard stories of what He did thousands of years ago, He is still alive today, relevant and involved in the affairs of men. If you let Him, He will reveal Himself to you. He will give you a future and a hope. You can experience a love you can't imagine, the love you've searched for all your life and didn't believe to exist.

People who are seeking God will find Him because He will make Himself known. People who are trying to accommodate their sin will find or create a religion they can accept. People who don't care about anything spiritual will find that God will reveal Himself to them but not force Himself upon them.

I remember the day I knew I was saved. In an instant I knew a love I couldn't describe. I had an insatiable desire to be close to God, to know everything about Him, to be in His presence and to worship Him with all my being.

I still want everyone to know Him like I know Him.

Sanctification

I was talking to the Lord one day and asked Him if He would go ahead and finish the sanctification process. I wanted to completely quit sinning. It had gotten to where He would forgive me before I even finished asking. I wanted to spend the rest of my life free from the temptation of sin.

Anyway I asked and He said no, He wouldn't do it. **He said if He were to free me from all sin, I would not finish learning what I needed to know about His mercy, grace and forgiveness.** I would start leaning on my own righteousness instead of His.

He's not surprised when I sin. He knew about every sin before I was born, paid the price for them all, and still accepts me. Does He love me less when I sin? His love for me is not based on me and my performance - it would never measure up.

His love is what defines Him.

There is nothing I can do or say to run Him off or make Him give up on me. He doesn't get mad at me. He doesn't push Himself on me or anyone either.

Don't misinterpret His mercy and grace as God taking a light stance on sin. The following is an excerpt of a conversation between God and David referring to David's son, Solomon:

> I will be a father to him and he will be a son to Me; when he commits iniquity, I will correct him with the rod of men and the strokes of the sons of men, [15] but My lovingkindness shall not depart from him...
>
> 2 Samuel 7:14-15

If you're getting beat up by the people you live or work with, ask the Lord if there is undealt-with sin in your life. Make no mistake, the Lord will not ignore our sin, but He's there for us to help in everything we do.

> For whom the Lord loves He reproves, Even as a father corrects the son in whom he delights.
>
> Proverbs 3:12

Back to the person who committed the grievous sin against me, you see Jesus was quick to forgive him. You might have noticed I was not. The Lord requires us to forgive just as freely as He does.

Forgiveness

It's been my experience that after someone gets saved, Jesus will clean up their act showing them areas of sin in their lives one by one in the order of importance to Him. I can remember saying, "Lord, you've never said anything about that before. I thought that wasn't really a sin."

We need to be quick to repent and quick to forgive.

Jesus ministered to the sinner. Some churches are better at creating an environment where anyone feels welcome, but that's not easy to do.

In some cases it can be harder to get into the local church than it is to get into heaven. Seekers find it easier to come into the church if we can't see their sin. But if it's obvious, we feel the need to clean them up before letting them in.

Let them come to Jesus. He is more than capable of cleaning and forgiving us. If we really want to save the world, then we need to get the church outside the four walls or better yet, let the world into our club.

People are pretty touchy about their pet sins. If we judge and reject them we might be condemning them to hell. But if we accept and forgive them just like they are - well, that could change the world.

> *Of Him all the prophets bear witness that through His name everyone who believes in Him receives forgiveness of sins."*
>
> *Acts 10:43*

Condensed Milk

4. Driving a Car off a Cliff

Driving back to Texas from Florida, there's a shortcut in Mississippi I take diagonally across the state between the interstates. It's much improved now, but the highway back then was a small two-lane road that wound through a heavily wooded area with rolling hills.

Just before dawn, I'd been driving for about eight hours and was very tired. Drinking coffee, driving with the window down, I was hoping the cold fresh air would keep me awake.

Suddenly I awoke! I'd fallen asleep and driven off the roadway. At first I couldn't see anything but a dark sky. Then I realized I was flying through the air. Unlike what you see in the movies, cars don't fly very well. With their engines in front, they're nose-heavy.

As the car started to nose down I could make out where I was. I was headed towards a tree in the bottom of a ravine. At this point I'm wide awake. My heart was beating rapidly. I tightened my grip on the steering wheel, locked my elbows straight and braced for impact. I took a last look at the tree approaching very rapidly and closed my eyes. I didn't want to watch.

They say that right before death your life passes before your eyes. Mine didn't; it occurred to me that no one knew I was there. I hadn't told anyone where I was going. It was going to be a surprise. I thought there's a good chance no one will even notice a wrecked car down here. They may not find me for a long time. People will think I just disappeared.

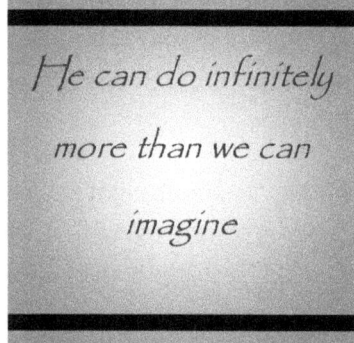

Well, it took me longer to think all this than it did for you to read it, and I started to think the same thing - I should've hit that tree by now. So what should I do? There's no way I'm going to open my eyes - that tree would be right there in my face. Maybe I missed the tree and I'm falling all the way to the bottom of the ravine. Even then I should have hit bottom by now.

I've got it! Maybe I'm still asleep and I'm just dreaming all this. No, I've never been more awake in my life.

My friend David Barron likes this part ... **if you've ever flown a car,** it's not the engine that makes all the noise. It's the tires. A car flying through the air is very quiet, the only sound you hear is of the wind rushing around the vehicle.

At this point I can't take it anymore. I'm about to open my eyes when suddenly I hear it. Faintly at first but getting louder and louder until yes! It's tire noise, like driving-down-the-middle-of-the-road tire noise. I open my eyes to find I'm driving down the road perfectly in my lane.

I brake hard and pull off the road, jump out of the car and yell, "Thank you, Jesus! Thank you, thank you, thank you, Jesus! Praise God!" For a while I just keep circling the car praising God, when I start to wonder ... how did I get back on the road?

I looked off the road, but it didn't look anything like what I had seen. Did I fall asleep and dream I drove off a cliff? Could be. I sure did drive a long time with my eyes closed, but God can probably do that. No, I decided I've never been more awake.

I turned around and drove back down the road looking off the shoulder for anything that looked like the tree in the ravine. As I back-tracked further and further south, the sun was coming up and nothing looked like I remembered.

I decided this was going to be one of those faith things. God wasn't going to let me know what He did; I was going to have to just trust and believe by faith. Was this all a dream? I decided it must have been.

I was about to give up the search when I came to a part of the road where, past the shoulder, the ground dropped off too steeply to see anything from the road. I stopped and got out of the car and walked over to the edge.

Condensed Milk

For a second I stopped breathing as I tried to take it all in. I was shocked to see the ravine and the tree, but most of all, to realize that you can't see them from the road!

I must have been awake ...

I thought, "What just happened? How did this happen? Did God do this? If so, how did He? Did an angel put the car back on the road? I should be dead ..."

Other trivia - the tree was so far back down the road, that not only did the Lord perform a miracle putting the car back on the road, but He also put it so far down the road that it would have had to travel faster than the car will go to end up where it did.

> *Now to Him who is able to do far more abundantly beyond all that we ask or think, according to the power that works within us,*
>
> Ephesians 3:20

Oh, by the way, did I tell you I still didn't believe God could do miracles like this at the time? I believed He could within the constraints of nature. But I didn't believe God could do anything outside the laws of physics.

This event happened very early in my relationship with the Lord, and I couldn't reconcile it. It took me four years to work through it. I discovered that God is all-powerful. The Lord can stretch your beliefs of what He can and will do.

5. The Big Greenhouse

This is just my speculation, but imagine: If God wanted to create beings like Him - capable of intelligence, capable of faith, hope and love, with a free will - how would He do it?

He created the angels. They knew Him, lived where He did. He loved them; He trained them. They needed no faith to believe in Him. Yet a third of them turned against Him.

Let's say God wanted to grow some spiritual beings. He could create a temporary body out of dust to house the eternal spirit He planned on maturing.

Where to put His creation?

Creating a round earth and putting it in the middle of space, **who but God could have dreamed that one up?** You can walk forever but you can't leave. It's like a giant playpen with no fence. Could it be the earth is a big greenhouse where God grows us in a controlled environment with reduced abilities, where the worst thing we can do is reject Him?

God created man in a day. When God created the angels they knew no sin. And we know a third of them fell when they discovered sin. When God created man, man too chose to sin against God. Therefore, God blesses us with the opportunity to be raised in our greenhouse fertilized with sin. When we graduate from this educational program called life, or redemption, we'll know full well the consequences of sin so that we will never rebel against Him again. Isn't an imperfect world a good place to teach someone about the consequences of sin and what separation from the Lord is like? Maybe we wouldn't forget that for all eternity. Is it possible that if the fallen angels had known the consequences of sin, maybe they wouldn't have fallen?

Right now He is managing the spiritual growth of seven billion souls in His greenhouse. Another significant group, those who have already passed into heaven, are with Him now enrolled in postgraduate studies pursuing continuing education.

When we're born, we don't know much, but no one has to teach us to sin. Yet from an early age we know we're meant for more. Do we miss what we don't know? Is the creator in our DNA more than we know? We dream of superheroes, flying, super powers, super strength. All these are attributes of God and angels but without the help of Holy Spirit, they're just out of our reach. God still created man in His image, but He chose to tone down our abilities. Only give us access to part of our brain, limit our strength, no walking through walls, teleporting, appearing and disappearing. Limit our ability to selfheal, little or no ESP.

Scientists have said if our brains worked the way they appear to be designed, we should be able to remember everything we see and hear. I asked the Lord why we can't. He said if we could recall all our sin at one time, it would be too much for us to bear. He has blessed us with forgetfulness.

They say at one time or other in our lives we all rebel. Do you suppose we all rebel against God? Is this part of the process too where we can rebel, repent and be forgiven so when we're in heaven we will never rebel again?

Then there's the pruning. The plant analogy really holds up here. The Lord used this to describe how He allows adversity in our lives to grow us up, to grow us closer to Him and to make us stronger. Pruning is never pleasant. If you haven't been pruned yet, **you will be.**

> *Every branch in Me that does not bear fruit, He takes away; and every branch that bears fruit, He prunes it so that it may bear more fruit.*
>
> *John 15:2*

Unlike the angels, we can't go directly to Him in bodily form (not at least without His help). By placing us in an environment where we have limited contact with Him, it builds our faith. He gave us His promises to build our hope. He sacrificed His Son to teach us about His love, and give us a way out of the greenhouse.

The only way to leave the greenhouse is to die. For those who believe, to be absent from our bodies is to be with Him. We have so much more to learn ... someday we will know the truth and the truth will set us free. For the plant wasn't created for the greenhouse nor was the greenhouse its final destination. Most plants spend a fraction of their life in a nursery. We will spend a fraction of eternity here.

Some people see this life here on earth as being everything. Compared to eternity, 120 years is nothing at all. Just as important for the rest of our lives are the comparatively brief years we spent in the education system. So it is for the time we spend here on earth. These years are important for teaching us the eternal purposes of God.

The thief on the cross didn't live long enough to accomplish any great ministry while he was alive here on earth. Then again his last few words still minister to us. (To have positive impact on anyone's life 2000 years after you've passed is quite an accomplishment). My point is, he only had minutes or hours to serve the Lord here on earth but he's had all this time to serve the Lord in heaven. Do you think God would say his was a wasted life?

We need to get eternity in our hearts. Maybe the prophesies in Scripture were also given to help get our eyes off our problems today, our life, our world, and help us see the Kingdom of God in the light of eternity. Maybe God is training us here for the next job. What's our next job? Maybe it's the thousand year reign. After the rapture you're going to have a righteous government that may need trained Christians to minister to the needs of the unsaved population. Just a guess.

> *Blessed and holy is the one who has a part in the first resurrection; over these the second death has no power, but they will be priests of God and of Christ and will reign with Him for a thousand years.*
>
> *Revelation 20:6*

Curious pieces in His greenhouse: Have you ever noticed, in order to live, we have to eat things that are or once were living? Is this a lesson in sacrifice? Have you ever noticed how the sun is so integral in the process of living things? G.K. Chesterton said, "God is like the sun; you cannot look at it, but without it, you cannot look at anything else."[D]

In the greenhouse analogy the role of the sun would be God. All life seems to come from the sun. Even the trees stretch out their leaves and seem to worship the sun. Did God create the sun to help us better understand who He is? We get most of our energy either directly or indirectly (fossil fuels) from the sun. Our environment, capable of supporting life, would not last long without the sun. Even the oxygen we need to breathe would quickly cease without it.

Scientists say the sun is a giant fusion reactor. They have been working since the 1950's to build one viable for commercial use. God made billions of these fusion reactors. We call them stars.

Many ancient civilizations worshiped the sun. It's easier for me to understand that than worshiping a statue. You think we have trouble with our image of God.

> *And beware not to lift up your eyes to heaven and see the sun and the moon and the stars, all the host of heaven, and be drawn away and worship them and serve them, those which the Lord your God has allotted to all the peoples under the whole heaven.*
>
> *Deuteronomy 4:19*

If God wanted to grow some spiritual beings, He might put them in a greenhouse where they would be safe under His watchful eye – a place where he could water us, tend us, and feed us as we grow, a place where He can protect us from life's storms. And when He is done and when it's time to leave the greenhouse, He might just take home with Him the most valuable thing He's ever created - His church.

6. The Prayer of a 12-Year-Old

It's amazing how God will answer the prayer of a little kid and not even a necessarily well thought out prayer. When I was about 12, living in Amarillo, Texas, our church youth group came down for a retreat at a church camp on Lake Dallas. It was cold and we had been staying inside the buildings, so I hadn't seen the lake.

I got up early one morning and went down to the water and was amazed at its beauty. It was just after dawn, as the fog was lifting off a smooth-as-glass surface. This lake was the most beautiful I had ever seen. **I prayed and asked the Lord if I could live on a lake like this someday.** I realized that where I lived in West Texas there wasn't much water. I thought it was a foolish request so I took it back. That was pretty much the end of it, and I forgot about the prayer.

Fifteen years later, I was married and had a family; a company offered me a job and we moved to the Dallas area. I kept looking for Lake Dallas but I couldn't find any lake with that name. I found the city of Lake Dallas, but no lake. Years later the Lord directed us to buy a piece of property a couple hundred feet from the shore of Lake Lewisville. I was surprised to find out the part of the lake we were building on was the old Lake Dallas which had

Condensed Milk

been renamed when they expanded the lake. I had been looking for the Christian camp; I knew roughly where it should be on the lake.

As the sun was setting one night my family and I had worked all day finishing the foundation of our new home. We were sitting on what would be the study (where I'm sitting now writing this) looking out across the lake. It had rained so the air was clear, and I spotted a cross on a building directly across the lake. It was the church camp I'd been looking for ... Camp Copass.

At that instant the Lord reminded me of the prayer I had prayed as a child. I just crumbled as I realized ... we were sitting on the very land I had looked upon those many years ago exactly on the other side of the lake.

Why did He do this? Why would it matter? This is a huge lake with miles and miles of shoreline. His attention to detail is off the scale. Maybe He was showing us how thoroughly He remembers our prayers. How important those prayers are to Him. By answering a ridiculously difficult-to-fulfill prayer of a child, He showed the depth of His love by answering it in ridiculous detail.

Since then we have visited Camp Copass, and one of the few things you can distinguish from anywhere on that part of the lake is the roof of our house sticking out of the trees.

Clearly the Lord hears and remembers our prayers.

7. The Church

Since the church is the body of Christ, have you ever noticed how all the hands hang out together? The eyes form their own church, the feet prefer the theology of feet and tongues say you're not saved unless you're a tongue. Just like a human body needs all its parts to function, so does the church. Each part has its strengths. It's hard for feet to grasp and throw a ball, just as it's hard to run fast on your hands.

Our beliefs grow as we grow in our understanding of God. Since we prefer to hang out with people that believe the way we do, we end up with a plethora of denominations (i.e. the aforementioned body parts).

Ephesians 4:11 describes the church as made up of the fivefold ministry: apostles, prophets, evangelists, pastors and teachers.

Some churches are good at catching, some cleaning, others help heal, yet there are churches whose main ministry is one of teaching and there are others which equip you for service. Some of the denominational churches, missionary churches and the seeker churches are good at catching (evangelism), while the Bible churches do a great job of teaching the Word. Some churches focus on physical and emotional healing. The Pentecostal, charismatic and non-doms often train people in the ministry of Holy Spirit and how to use spiritual gifts. A lot of great worship music came out of these churches. There are prophetic churches that listen for a fresh word from the Lord and make that word available to the Body. Apostolic churches often minister to other churches. Then there are specialty churches like those that pray and worship 24/7. There are even biker churches and cowboy churches, etc.

Some people stay in the same church their whole life. But often the Lord takes us progressively through different ministries to train us or to have us train others.

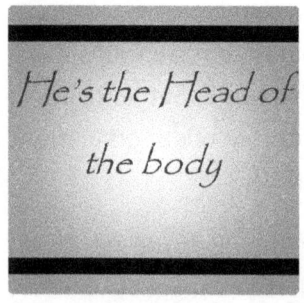

It's almost like school. We start out in kindergarten and proceed to elementary, middle school, then high school, college, etc. As the Lord leads us to leave one church and proceed to the next, it's not necessarily a bad thing. Keep in mind the Lord hates divorce and we shouldn't get offended and leave a church, but seek Him first and He will lead us where He wants us to be. Don't be surprised when He determines you have learned what He wanted you to learn or you served where He wanted you to serve and now it's time to move on to the next church.

In the same way the Lord extends grace to us even when we're fools, let us extend grace to other believers on any issue where the Word of God is not clear. I think it's possible that the truth of God, His theology, may just be too big for us to grasp in one lifetime. Maybe all we can grasp is a piece of it, and clearly the Lord is not leading us all to expertise in the same teachings. Yet the core beliefs, the most important truths, are fairly consistent throughout the church.

Could it be a problem with the Church is that instead of leading people to encounters with the living God (i.e. Jesus's miracles), we innocently become God for the people? For example, instead of the miraculous feeding of the 5000, we start a food bank program where very well-meaning, godly people collect food and redistribute it to the poor. **Does that introduce the poor to the living God as well as the miracle did?**

I know the Lord works with what we have, and I don't think we should shut down any food banks, but if we could follow the Lord's lead, do His will, minister more like He did, maybe we could help them to meet the living God, to lead them to His living water, to help them discover His saving grace. Wouldn't that be better than caring for the needy their whole lives just for them to die lost in the end?

Right now most of the church's resources go to buildings and staff. Very little makes it to the poor, widows and orphans. Unfortunately, we've relegated that to the state and yet ministering to the widows and orphans is how He describes His religion.

> *Pure and undefiled religion in the sight of our God and Father is this: to visit orphans and widows in their distress, and to keep oneself unstained by the world.*
>
> *James 1:27*

Another example: Let's say we see a man standing at the street corner with a sign "Homeless - need food." We stop and give him some money as a good Christian giving to the poor. He takes the money and buys alcohol, gets drunk, then sobers up in time to make it back out to the corner again the next day. But let's suppose we didn't give him anything and instead he hits bottom and cries out to God and is radically saved. Without knowing God's will, we could cause more harm than good.

We need - the church needs - to partner with God and be His hands and feet, to obey His commands, to seek His direction - because then and only then will we, the church, be truly successful. I need to die to self, so no longer I live, but Jesus Christ lives in/through me. I need to quit trying to control people's actions and love them instead.

Give them all to God; trust Him to do His will in their lives. Pray, listen and be ready to move in their lives on His command.

8. Speaking in Tongues

My first experience with tongues was not a good one. Some friends of ours had gone to a church where they were taught the way a person receives the gift of tongues or learned to speak in tongues would be to take some nonsensical phrases and repeat them over and over. If you repeated them in faith then the Lord would give you the gift of tongues.

And you know, that may be all well and good. I don't think at the time that I had the faith or the theology to deal with that very well or the grace to trust the Lord to teach me. Every time my friend spoke in tongues he said the same phrase over and over again. I got to where I had it memorized and could say it as well he did. It was annoying.

Later on when I started seeking spiritual gifts, I told the Lord that I would be happy if He gave me all the rest of the spiritual gifts. Since speaking in tongues is so controversial, well, He could just keep that one and I would be okay with that. After all it's only a temporary gift as we won't need tongues in heaven.

> *Love never fails; but if there are gifts of prophecy, they will be done away; if there are tongues, they*

will cease; if there is knowledge, it will be done away. ⁹ For we know in part and we prophesy in part; ¹⁰ but when the perfect comes, the partial will be done away.

1 Corinthians 13:8-10

Years ago Nan Bagby was sharing part of her testimony.[E] Nan had come to know the Lord later in her life and was new to the things of the Spirit. One day she was in a church service singing, minding her own business.

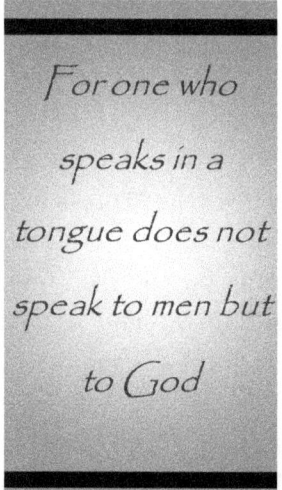

For one who speaks in a tongue does not speak to men but to God

Suddenly she started worshiping God in a language she didn't know. She was so elated in the spirit and happy. Nan kept speaking in an unknown tongue until finally she went to the women's rest room and started to kind of panic because she thought somehow maybe she couldn't or wouldn't be able to speak English anymore. But after a few minutes everything returned to normal.

She had never heard of tongues before, had no idea the gift existed or knew anything about it. When she found out what the phenomenon was called and asked other people about it, she learned that she had received the gift of tongues. Nan's testimony really impacted me and it also gave tongues some credibility.

And they were all filled with the Holy Spirit and began to speak with other tongues, as the Spirit was giving them utterance.

Acts 2:4

Jumping ahead a few years, we were sitting in a leadership meeting. I was very tired and having a hard time staying awake. Afterwards, we were going directly from the meeting to a church service.

In the little gap between, an incredible man of God, Nick Irons, came over and said, "Let's go get a cup of coffee." He knew who I was but we were by no means close. I knew he was a strong Christian, and it was a great opportunity to have a cup of coffee with an awesome man of God.

Even though the church service was about to start, I felt like it was important to do. We went and got a cup of coffee and came back to the church parking lot finishing the cup when he said, **"You have a problem with tongues, don't you?"** I told him he was right, I did have a problem with tongues.

Nick used a military analogy. He said if a soldier was trying to call headquarters in battle and tell them that they were running low on ammunition, they wouldn't broadcast it on a radio frequency that the enemy could hear. That could be bad for them. They would use an encrypted radio channel so that their conversation would be secure.

Nick said that was similar to how tongues worked. When we pray in English to the Lord and list all of our problems and our issues, we could be broadcasting that information to any spiritual enemy that might be listening at the time. Where if that's communicated in tongues, it's like praying using an encrypted channel but it's much more than that.

Our spirit communicates with the Lord using words and communicating emotion that we don't have the words to say or even the conscious knowledge to communicate. I said, "I never thought of it that way. Maybe tongues is a good thing."

Nick asked if I wanted to receive the gift of tongues and he offered to pray for me right there in the car, in the middle of the parking lot. He prayed and almost immediately I felt something rising up from inside the center of my chest and coming out and exploding out of my mouth - tons of words in an unknown language. It seemed important to say them and important for the words to be said. It felt like I had been mute all my life and that suddenly I was able to speak. It went on for some time.

I was wearing contacts, and one of them popped out and flipped across the car. Nick was trying to find it, but I didn't care. This was just too cool and then as quickly as it started everything that needed to be said was said and it was over. There was a moment there where I thought, "I may never be able to speak English again." Then the next thought I had was, "Who cares? This is as good as it gets!"

Several days later I was praying and asking the Lord about it. It was a phenomenal experience, and He said it would be kind of similar to if all of a sudden your dog was able to speak English. We would have so much that we would want to say to each other that we hadn't ever been able to say.

Years later I was in a life group meeting at the Haun's house. There were a lot of people there; some that I knew well, some that I didn't know at all. At the end of the meeting there was a man who asked for prayer. He was career military and had been back in a civilian job for a couple of years.

Our life group pastor and good friend Ricky Haun asked me and several other men to come over and pray for him. I felt about as spiritual as a brick that evening and didn't really want to pray for him. Ricky encouraged me to pray anyway (when we are weak, He is strong), so I stood by while everybody else prayed. When everybody else was finished it was my turn to pray, and I started praying in English. That only lasted for a few seconds then a powerfully strong presence of the Lord came.

Suddenly, this Oriental-sounding tongue was coming out of my mouth with such authority - very demanding, very loud

Condensed Milk

and very hard. Quite a lot was said, and then suddenly something broke in the spirit and everything was really peaceful and calm. I quit speaking.

Prayer time was over, and the man stood up and said, "Thank you for the prayer. I really needed that." He turned and looked at me and said, "Where did you learn to speak Korean?" He said the reason he was asking for prayer was related to the years he spent serving in Korea. I said, "I don't speak Korean." He said, "Well, you sure were." I asked him, "What did I say in Korean?" He said I was going way too fast for him. He said, "I just know enough of the language to be able to get around. I could pick out a word here and there, but you were speaking Korean like a native." Isn't God amazing?

> *These signs will accompany those who have believed: in My name they will cast out demons, they will speak with new tongues;*
>
> *Mark 16:17*

Peculiar trend ... there were several ladies visiting our church from an Asian country. They asked for prayer but couldn't speak much English, and we didn't know what they needed prayer for, so we started praying for them in tongues. When we finished praying for them, one of the ladies smiled and started speaking to us in an unintelligible language and was very surprised that we didn't understand her. As her English was not very good it took a little while to deduce that she spoke Korean and couldn't understand how after I had just finished praying for her in Korean that I didn't understand what she was saying!

That had to be more bizarre for her than it was for me. I wonder what I said?

> So then tongues are for a sign, not to those who believe but to unbelievers; but prophecy is for a sign, not to unbelievers but to those who believe.
>
> 1 Corinthians 14:22

We were hosting a small group meeting in our house. During the meeting I turned to speak to Jan, one of the ladies in our group. When I started to say her name, "Mishchah" (meesh-khaw') came out of my mouth. I was embarrassed. I focused to say her name clearly. As I concentrated to say her name correctly, "Mishchah" came out again. In the spirit it felt like that was really her name. I apologized and tried to explain what I thought had happened. I think it was a spiritual name for her. Anyway, later on I looked it up in a Concordance. It's Hebrew: מִשְׁחָה. It's a feminine noun and means "anointed." The name really fit her well.

As time goes on I have discovered that sometimes you can understand the meaning of the words spoken in tongues and translate it on the fly. I've also noticed that the words said in the tongue don't appear to come from your head but from your spirit. Often I've had a whole conversation with myself in my head while my mouth is busy speaking the tongue. I only need my brain to pause and take a breath. Similar to prophetic words that originate in your spirit and not your head, it's very hard to remember what was said. Both you and the person receiving the word are hearing it for the first time, at the same time.

Some people say if you can't speak in tongues you're not filled with the Spirit. I received the gift of tongues a week after I was filled with the Spirit. I've not seen anyone gifted with tongues though that was not already Spirit-filled.

> *When Paul placed his hands on them, the Holy Spirit came on them, and they spoke in tongues and prophesied.*
>
> *Acts 19:6*

It seems that often the words spoken in the tongue are so important and necessary and therefore vitally need to be said. I don't know why. I've noticed some words are Hebrew, Greek, French, Spanish and German. And who knows what else. Scripture says sometimes it's the language of angels.

I've also discovered that you can sing in tongues. God has blessed us with this gift. We need to be more open to the good gifts God is willing to bless us with.

I think something should be said about the most controversial use of tongues when this gift is used in a church service. Few pastors appreciate this use of the gift and would prefer the congregation to abstain from speaking. Still some churches embrace the use of tongues in their services. One person will speak in a tongue and another will give the interpretation.

> *If anyone speaks in a tongue, it should be by two or at the most three, and each in turn, and one must interpret; [28] but if there is no interpreter, he must keep silent in the church; and let him speak to himself and to God.*
>
> 1 Corinthians 14:27-28

Condensed Milk

9. Runaway Love

When I was 8 years old, I thought my parents didn't love me so I decided to leave home forever. I ran away from home. After many miles and hours, I decided I still loved my parents. I was convinced they didn't love me but thought maybe my love for them was stronger than their disdain for me. I turned around and returned home, committed to love them whether they ever loved me in return or not.

> *For if you love those who love you, what reward do you have? Do not even the tax collectors do the same?*
>
> *Matthew 5:46*

The Lord told me recently that was what He loves most about me. You know, that's how He is. He loves so. Many people never even know how much He loves, how much He's done for them, how much He's sacrificed for them.

Lord, I have known for quite a while about the place in my heart that only You can fill, but I cried with joy when you told me how You have a place in your heart only I can fill.

Condensed Milk

It's funny though, I've discovered no matter how full your heart is with love, it's like it has a leak or maybe it's a consumable. Sooner or later you need a recharge.

Spending time with the Lord, I saw that no one can make someone that knows them love them in return. You can't force someone to love you. Even God won't make someone love Him. If someone doesn't love you, nothing you can do or say makes much difference. You have to open up your heart and let them in.

Love comes from relationship. Even after all the Lord has done to prove His love, you have to know Him to love Him. You can't really love someone you don't know. He commands us to pray, and we do. In prayer time comes relationship. In relationship you can fall in love. To know Him is to love Him.

> Whoever confesses that Jesus is the Son of God, God abides in him, and he in God. [16] We have come to know and have believed the love which God has for us. God is love, and the one who abides in love abides in God, and God abides in him. [17] By this, love is perfected with us, so that we may have confidence in the day of judgment; because as He is, so also are we in this world.
>
> 1 John 4:15-17

Have you ever been apart from a loved one, waiting to hear from them, counting the days and hours till you are together again? Does our Lord wait to hear from us? Do we long to be with Him? Do we know Him well enough to miss Him? What do you know about Him? What's His favorite color? Do you share your hopes, your dreams, your fears with Him?

He told me once, **"I put dreams into the hearts of men."** Imagine that, God sometimes puts dreams into our hearts. Then He helps make them come true, knowing how this will bless us, grow us, mature us, draw us closer to Him. Maybe He does it as an expression of His love. He says to delight yourself in the Lord and He will give you the desires of your heart.

> *Love is patient, love is kind and is not jealous; love does not brag and is not arrogant, ⁵ does not act unbecomingly; it does not seek its own, is not provoked, does not take into account a wrong suffered,*
>
> *1 Corinthians 13:4-5*

By the way, upon return from my little adventure, as I neared home, I could see a police car parked in front of my house. I thought this is going to be bad. I took a deep breath and continued toward home. I was committed to return no matter the cost. I walked in the front door, Mom picked me up and hugged me and told me how much she loved me. Who'd a thought? That was not the reaction I

Condensed Milk

expected. This was my first experience with unconditional love and forgiveness. Every time I see her and Dad now they tell me how much they love me and how proud they are of me. I never get tired of hearing that. Mom and Dad - I love you so much. Thanks for putting up with me.

Good story, but what really happened? Are you ready for a peak behind the curtain?

As I contemplated what happened here, I had to ask myself, where was God in all of this? Is He going to stand by and watch a little kid run away from home? There's no way this would have turned out good. And where did an eight-year-old suddenly gain the wisdom to grasp the concept of unconditional love?

He puts dreams in our hearts. That's not all God does. He watches, and He waits. If the adversity won't produce His desired result then our loving Father God intervenes. He loves us enough to watch over us 24 hours a day. He loves us so much He makes little corrections from time to time. Some make no obvious difference. Some make a big difference. For example, He might stick a car back on the road when someone falls asleep driving.

How great is God's love, and yet I've thought, "Nobody loves me." If I could only grasp how great is this love that never stops watching over me, protecting me, not caring whether I know or not. Talk about love! Talk about God's runaway love …

10. Praying for the Nations

Years ago someone prophesied Alison and I would pray for the nations. We laughed. You have to understand that at the time we had barely been out of Texas. Although we had lived in Florida for a short period of time, we had never been outside the country, didn't have passports and had only been to a handful of other states.

> *Tell of His glory among the nations, His wonderful deeds among all the peoples.*
>
> Psalm 96:3

A large group of people from our church went to Toronto for training, and we were blessed to be able to go with them. We were going to be trained by the ministry team that had ministered the Toronto Blessing almost every night for a year.

When we arrived in Toronto at the Airport Church, their ministry team decided we knew enough already and they were going to take the rest of the week off.[F] It'd been months since they'd had a break. At the end of the evening instead of praying for people in groups of five, they took Alison and me to a line of maybe 75 to 100 people and told us to pray for all those people.

This was really out of our comfort zone. We were new on the ministry team and had never prayed for strangers before. As I walked up to the first man in line, I prayed silently, "Lord, the way I see this, it's my responsibility to stand here, stretch out my hand and pray for these people. It's Your responsibility for all the rest."

Alison had a little notebook and we asked each person what their prayer need was and where they were from, and she would write it down.

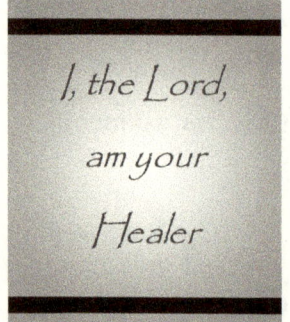

I hadn't learned to pray for people with my eyes open yet so I would close my eyes and start praying. I could feel the strong sweet presence of the Lord in the room. I could feel the power of God on my hand. I could feel the power of God flowing through my body reaching into the spirits of these people and healing their hearts, healing their bodies, making them whole.

We had catchers standing behind the people being prayed for in case they might fall out under the power of the Spirit. I would stand there and pray with my eyes closed and my hand over their head without touching them. There was no sensation nor did I have any awareness of when they would fall out in the Spirit. Alison would gently touch me on the shoulder and tell me, "Honey, they're on the floor."

Now to Him who is able to do far more abundantly beyond all that we ask or think, according to the power that works within us,

Ephesians 3:20

We prayed for a lot of people. We learned a lot about the ministry of Holy Spirit.

We were even attacked by a demonic spirit. I was so upset by it I didn't want to pray for anybody anymore. I asked the Lord what He was going to do about it. He asked me why I was there. I told Him I was there to pray for people. He said go do it then.

Apparently He didn't consider the demonic spirit a threat. Later after one simple prayer the spirit was gone. What an amazing week. I could write a whole book on what I saw and what the Lord taught me that week.

At the end of the week Alison and I were shopping in a souvenir store to find something to bring back for our children. She found a T-shirt with the flags of the nations on it. It had approximately 30 to 40 flags on it.

Suddenly she stopped and had this shocked expression on her face. She said, **"Look at the order of the flags."** She pulled out her little notebook and compared the countries of the people we had prayed for to the flags on the shirt.

The flags were printed on the shirt in the same order as the nationalities of the people we prayed for. What a

Condensed Milk

coincidence - or if that was God, and I believe it was - what attention to detail!

We prayed for people from every major nation on the earth.

We prayed for people from nations we hadn't even heard of and became fast friends.

God gave us a heart for the nations.

> "I am the Lord, I have called You in righteousness, I will also hold You by the hand and watch over You, And I will appoint You as a covenant to the people, As a light to the nations,
>
> *Isaiah 42:6*

11. Sticking Pennies to the Wall

None of us have trouble believing in what God can do; we have trouble believing in what He will do.

I was praying with a heavy heart.

Is it because I lacked faith? No, I know He can.

Is it because I think He won't, or at least not as soon as I would hope?

Is that faith or bullying God to do my will? Am I trying to make my world perfect? He is succeeding in perfecting me.

One day the Lord said, "If I answer every question you ask, where's the faith in that?" Could it be we're supposed to be learning how to better operate in faith?

Our friends the Tripodes had just come back from a conference at Bethel Church in Redding, California.[G] They told us of all the awesome things God had done and what they had learned.

On a humorous note, they told how they saw some young people in the corner laughing. Their curiosity got the best of them and they went over to see what they were doing. They were sticking pennies to the wall! It started as a faith exercise. Ryan Tripode went on to tell how even his five year old would stick a penny on the wall and ask Holy Spirit to hold it there and it would stick!

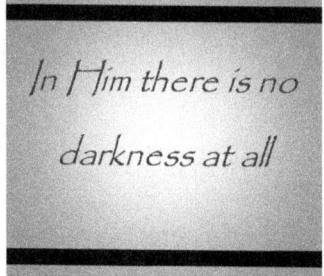
In Him there is no darkness at all

> And He said to them, "Because of the littleness of your faith; for truly I say to you, if you have faith the size of a mustard seed, you will say to this mountain, 'Move from here to there,' and it will move; and nothing will be impossible to you.
>
> Matthew 17:20

Even nonbelievers have asked the Lord to stick coins to the wall and they have stayed. In Mark 9:38 the disciples complained to Jesus that people were performing acts of faith who were not following Jesus. Could it be faith is faith whether you believe in God or not?

We went home and couldn't wait until we could try it. We were so excited. We got a pile of pennies and started holding them to the wall and asking Holy Spirit, "Would You please stick this penny to the wall?" After trying most

Sticking Pennies to the Wall

of the night the best my family experienced was a couple of seconds stuck to the wall.

I pulled up YouTube videos of people sticking pennies to walls, doors, windows, even on the glass.[H] Finally I put a penny on my forehead and asked Holy Spirit if He would hold the penny to my head. **I was amazed it stuck!** We got such a kick out of it.

The crazy thing is you can lean over or shake your head back and forth real fast and not only would the penny not come off your forehead but you could feel it like it had little bitty legs trying to hang on; it would pull itself in tighter to your head. Even now, there are times when it will only stay on for seconds or not at all. Then again I've driven all the way to work with a coin on my forehead.

I know, I know, this one's a little out there - even for me.

Things I've noticed: We've not experienced this at all without some presence of the Lord. We found that pennies tend to stick to people who are most open to the ministry of the Spirit.

I've not detected anything dark or demonic about this. At first it did seem a bit New Age-y to me.

God does some bizarre things. I haven't seen the gold dust but I have heard about it. I've heard about the glory clouds and the feathers. Kinda like manna ...

Condensed Milk

I've approached this very scientifically and there's nothing mechanical, electrical or chemical that's holding these coins to the wall - at least in most cases. Something supernatural is holding it to the wall.

Is it God or is it a demonic force? If it's a demonic force, their marketing needs help because God's getting the glory for it. If the Lord doesn't want us doing this, I found He's more than capable of correcting me when I do things outside His will.

Most miracles in Scripture meet needs that can't easily be met. I couldn't find many scriptures for a miracle or act of faith like sticking pennies that only increased faith and served no other purpose. I think walking on water would be one, after all Jesus could have gone across the sea in the boat the disciples were in. Maybe some of the plagues of Moses qualify. The changing of water into wine, the net full of fish or the Fig tree might count.

An attribute of faith is that exercising faith builds faith. But it seems that no matter how strong your faith is and no matter how many times you've moved successfully in the things of the Spirit, you can't predict the outcome. It's not like practice makes perfect. It definitely helps, but we can't gain some skill that allows us to use spiritual gifts flawlessly every time from that point on. There is an element in all this that involves God's will. You can't know that God is always going to do the same thing and you will have the same result.

We can't presume upon God. Moving successfully in the Spirit requires God's participation. It must be in accordance with His will, for His purposes and still include our faith for us to be successful in the Kingdom of God. Our God is consistent but not easily predictable.

Being successful in the Kingdom of God is about partnering with God to accomplish His purposes and requires our relationship with Him to be strong as well as our faith.

Sticking pennies to the wall has really increased my faith. I pray for all kinds of things that I never did before. Yet I still don't seem to have the faith of a mustard seed. I don't know about you, but I haven't heard of anyone casting mountains in the sea lately. So, if sticking pennies to the wall will get us where we need to be, even though it might be considered foolish, I'm for one willing to be more foolish than this.

> *Truly I say to you, whoever says to this mountain, 'Be taken up and cast into the sea,' and does not doubt in his heart, but believes that what he says is going to happen, it will be granted him.*
>
> Mark 11:23

Condensed Milk

12. Trusting God

I spend a lot time praying about problems and circumstances that I cannot solve. The focus of the prayer often is on me, work, family or friends. Many seemingly unresolvable issues I pray about over and over, trying to persuade God to do my will. Time would be better spent seeking His will, resting in Him, trusting God. I need to spend less time whining and more time sitting at His feet listening, learning. I need to focus less on the problems and more on the One who knew all the problems I would face before I was born. I need to spend less time seeking His hand and more time seeking His face.

> Trust in the Lord and do good;
> Dwell in the land and cultivate faithfulness.
> [4] Delight yourself in the Lord;
> And He will give you the desires of your heart.
> [5] Commit your way to the Lord,
> Trust also in Him, and He will do it.
> Psalm 37:3-5

Trusting in the Lord is difficult because we are used to trusting in ourselves. We want or need to be in control. Trusting the Lord requires us to turn over control to Him, to lean on Him and not on our own understanding.

Condensed Milk

> *The steps of a man are established by the Lord,*
> *And He delights in his way.*
> *²⁴ When he falls, he will not be hurled headlong,*
> *Because the Lord is the One who holds his hand.*
>
> Psalm 37:23-24

Where is the line between what we do and what He makes happen? It's difficult for me to trust Him with my future. There's this passage (Matthew 6:25-33) where Jesus says not to worry about having enough food or drink, that God provides for the birds and He will take care of you too.

Have you looked at the birds? It's amazing they survive. They wake up every day looking for food and don't know where their next meal will come. If God takes care of the birds, how in the world could I not trust Him to take care of me?

Jesus says, "You of little faith!"

Your heavenly Father knows you need all these things. Do you think your Father is going to let you starve to death?

I have trust issues, so my honest answer is - yes! I think it's a distinct possibility.

See, to Jesus in this passage, us being taken care of is a no-brainer. What's wrong with me - I don't see it that way. Am I the only one struggling with this? I know there are situations where people starve to death. But I don't have any friends or family members that have starved to death -

so the Lord must be doing a good job of caring for our needs. And yet I'm worried that I might not be able to make ends meet sometimes or have enough funds to retire.

If I really trusted God, I would see this as a no-brainer. If I trusted Him, really trusted Him, I would see - He's got this.

Do I trust You?

You created the ground upon which I stand
You created the air I breathe
You created the water I drink
You created the food I eat
You created me
You created my family
You've kept me alive
You've trained me to do my job
You told me where to work
You told me who to marry
You have given us plans, projects, direction
You said everything would be ok
You are my strong tower
You've proven Your love
You are my Shepherd
You said I would not be ashamed
You are my salvation
You are my light
If God is for me - who can be against me

Why is it so hard to trust You, Lord?

Condensed Milk

Trust in the Lord with all your heart and do not lean on your own understanding. ⁶ In all your ways acknowledge Him, and He will make your paths straight.

Proverbs 3:5-6

He says, "Do not fear." Is it true if we were to trust Him then maybe all the bad things that we feared would happen all our lives wouldn't happen? He says He causes blessing to fall on the just and the unjust. Maybe He blesses us whether we trust Him or not.

Maybe the main difference is "the just" enjoy peace that comes from trusting God. Is it possible the future isn't as dark as it sometimes appears? He says not to worry about tomorrow. He says not to fret; it leads only to evil.

Have you noticed how few bad things really do happen, at least a lot less than we feared would?

I should not lean on my understanding - maybe I should trust Him. I need to know in the core of my being that if God is for me who can be against me. That even the few bad things that happen, My Lord, out of His compassion and great love for me, allows them so that all things come together for good for those who love the Lord. Trust Him; just do it.

When I am afraid, I will put my trust in You.

Psalm 56:3

The Lord says it is easier to trust Him if we understand who we are in Christ Jesus.

If you ask me, "Who are you?" I might tell you what I do for a living. I might tell you about my family. I might even tell you I'm a Christian, but I probably wouldn't tell you I am a child of God. Yet we are so much more in Christ Jesus.

We are sons of God! We have direct access to the throne, we are seated with Christ in heavenly places, and we are joint heirs with Christ!

> *But as many as received Him, to them He gave the right to become children of God, even to those who believe in His name,*
>
> *John 1:12*
>
> *and if children, heirs also, heirs of God and fellow heirs with Christ, if indeed we suffer with Him so that we may also be glorified with Him.*
>
> *Romans 8:17*

If I can get this in my heart, I'm not just a number or a servant but a son. As a father, I know what an earthly father will do for a son. How much more will my heavenly Father care for me, protect me, love me.

Condensed Milk

For you are all sons of God through faith in Christ Jesus.

Galatians 3:26

Maybe it's hard to trust a generic god. But it should be easier to trust a personal Savior, the Lord, my King and my Father God. If I can get this right, if I can be aware of whose I am, it could be life changing.

I purpose to trust you, Lord.

13. I Come Quickly

One day I had been praying and really seeking an answer from the Lord about a situation that was going on at the office. I honestly don't remember what the crisis was, but I was upset and demanding an answer from God, or more specifically, from Jesus. I had been trying to get to know God and to differentiate between the persons of God, so I wanted Jesus to answer my question.

I was operating off of this scripture:

> *Ask, and it will be given to you; seek, and you will find; knock, and it will be opened to you. [8] For everyone who asks receives, and he who seeks finds, and to him who knocks it will be opened. [9] Or what man is there among you who, when his son asks for a loaf, will give him a stone? [10] Or if he asks for a fish, he will not give him a snake, will he? [11] If you then, being evil, know how to give good gifts to your children, how much more will your Father who is in heaven give what is good to those who ask Him!*
>
> Matthew 7:7-11.

I felt like the Lord owed me. I pulled a chair out into the center of the living room and decided I was going to sit there and pray until He gave me an answer. And I wasn't going to move until He did.

Alison decided I needed time alone with God. She took the children and they went off to do some other activity until I had a chance to work through this.

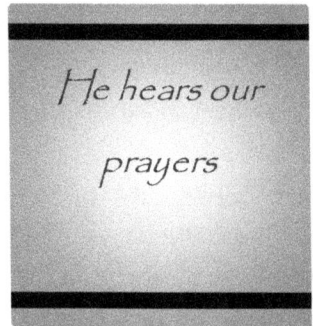

They left and I sat in the chair, and I sat in the chair, and I sat in the chair. As the afternoon went by and it started getting dark, I refused to even get up out of the chair to turn the lights on. I was determined that I was going to wait Him out.

All of a sudden the presence of the Lord was in the room. The room got so holy that I wanted and needed to take my shoes off, and I fell on my face in the presence of the Lord.

Not really being a person that ever understood the taking of shoes off and falling on your face, it was not a normal reaction for me. Yet there was the need inside me that I can't describe. I needed desperately to remove my shoes and get my face as close to the floor as possible.

The power, the holiness that was in the room; I was aware that I was a man of unclean lips. I remembered the passage in Isaiah.

Then I said, "Woe is me, for I am ruined! Because I am a man of unclean lips, And I live among a people of unclean lips; For my eyes have seen the King, the Lord of hosts."

Isaiah 6:5

I was aware in this presence of His holiness, of my lack. I was trying to get as low and as close to the floor as I could possibly get. I was shrinking back, and there was a real fear.

A few seconds passed by and I heard a loud voice, powerful and authoritative; so much so, that it seemed like it would break bones or shatter trees, but it didn't hurt me. I don't know if it was an audible voice or if I just heard it in my head. It sounded like an audible voice to me.

The Lord said slowly, "**I COME QUICKLY!**" That's all He said.

I sat there in silence.

The presence of the Lord in the room lifted slowly, and the room returned to normal. He didn't really answer my question, but maybe He had. My problem at work didn't really matter anymore.

Later I noticed the last words Jesus says in Revelation are very similar (the last red letter words).

> *He who testifies to these things says, "Yes, I am coming quickly." Amen. Come, Lord Jesus.*
>
> *Revelation 22:20*

It's interesting the way God stated the phrase I heard in my living room, it seemed to communicate past, present and future tense. As in, "I have come quickly, I do come quickly and I will come quickly." Also, it occurred to me that it was probably said by Lord Jesus, as Holy Spirit is already here and (as far as I know) the Father's not coming.

This whole experience need not to have happened if I was relating correctly to Jesus. See, He is my King and the Lord of my life. Like Sir Lancelot who searched far and wide for a king worthy of his sword, we have found One, or He has found us. We should take our queues from Him. Let Him guide and direct us. I know many people deal with conflict at work by simply not caring. They say, "I was looking for a job when I found this one." What they are really saying is, "I don't care about others; I care only about myself." That's not an option for a Christian.

The Lord commands us to care.
The Lord commands us to serve.
The Lord commands us to be forgiving.
The Lord commands us to be diligent.

Our goal can't be to do all we do to please men. Our goal must be to do what we do to please God. Because no matter how hard we try, we'll never be able to keep man happy. We are working for the Lord.

> Whatever you do, do your work heartily, as for the Lord rather than for men, [24] knowing that from the Lord you will receive the reward of the inheritance. It is the Lord Christ whom you serve.
>
> Colossians 3:23-24

We shouldn't worry about our problems at work or at home. I shouldn't have let things get to me.

> *Cease from anger and forsake wrath;*
> *Do not fret; it leads only to evildoing.*
>
> Psalm 37:8

We need to rest in Him and wait patiently for Him. I'm not supposed to gain my self-worth from my work or my employer. I shouldn't try to bolster my self-esteem from other people's accolades. He should be my source of affirmation.

The Lord tells me to rest in Him, to not worry about tomorrow, to trust in Him, to commit my ways to Him. I shouldn't be so demanding, pressuring Him to solve all my problems. I should be praying to Him and seeking His direction, let Him direct my paths. The Lord says He directs our steps and that He will never leave or abandon us.

> *The mind of man plans his way,*
> *But the Lord directs his steps.*
>
> Proverbs 16:9

Condensed Milk

> *Make sure that your character is free from the love of money, being content with what you have; for He Himself has said, "I will never desert you, nor will I ever forsake you,"*
>
> *Hebrews 13:5*

We have authority in Jesus Christ as priests and sons of the living God. We should be ministers of reconciliation, peacemakers. We should arrive at work every day in the full armor of God, by the power of God, with intentions to do the best job we can as unto the Lord.

14. The Trinity

For the longest time I just prayed to God. I was not really aware of any difference in the members of the Godhead. Even the few times God spoke to me I couldn't tell who was speaking.

Upon being Spirit-filled, I became close to Holy Spirit. He was all the God I could ever need. I actually became addicted to His presence, and I would spend huge chunks of my day trying to stay as long as I could in His presence.

He showed me spiritual gifts and how and when to use them. We ministered a lot together. Sometimes His presence was so strong I thought He would break my body.

He taught me so much, but then it was time and He pointed me to Jesus. Jesus almost immediately pointed me to Father God.

> *Go therefore and make disciples of all the nations, baptizing them in the name of the Father and the Son and the Holy Spirit,*
>
> *Matthew 28:19*

I was always scared of Father God. I thought He turned people into pillars of salt. But I spent a lot of time with Him. I got to know Him and I grew to love Him. As I write this and think of Him, I tear up. The depths of His love, He became Abba God (Daddy God) to me.

He has an incredible sense of humor. With Jesus being King and Holy Spirit the Comforter, Father God is a little more laid back. It wasn't too long before He pointed me back to Jesus.

Most of my time now is spent with Lord Jesus. He is my King and my Lord and my days are spent trying to learn more about Him and the Kingdom of God, following His lead and trying to listen to Him and obey His commands.

I was talking to the Lord about how I get wrapped up in life and go long periods without being aware of Him so much so that I mistakenly think He doesn't care or know what's going on in my life.

The Lord said, "I'm with you all the time; I told you I will never leave or abandon you. I'm more involved in your life than you are aware."

I may not always be in His presence but He's always present with me. He's with me everywhere I go and everything I do and still loves me.

15. Falling Out in the Spirit

Our church staff had returned from visiting a church up in Toronto. The service was very different that day. There were people laughing, there were people that appeared to be drunk, and they started sharing testimony after testimony about this revival going on in Toronto. At the end of the service they invited people up for prayer.

I can't explain why but from my customary seat two rows from the back of the church I went straight up to the front and was second in line. About a dozen church staff and ministry team members were praying for people. I watched while I waited in the line of someone I knew and trusted as he prayed for the person in front of me. People were falling out in the Spirit left and right all around me. They were pulling the chairs back out of the way so there was room for more people on the floor.

At that time in my life, I had heard of the term "slain in the Spirit" and knew what it meant but I had never actually seen anyone be slain in the Spirit or fall out in the Spirit and lay down on the floor.

It was a little bit scary. I prayed and put the Lord on notice, and I told Him that I didn't want there to be an insincere bone in my body. If He wanted me on the floor, He was going to have to knock me off my feet. I wasn't going to go down easy. (For that challenge I would get to go down on concrete without a catcher.)

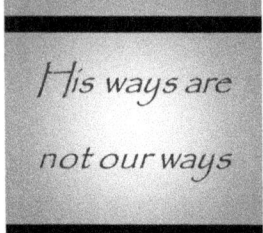

As my friend prayed for me I fought successfully to stay on my feet. A few minutes later I was standing behind Alison as they prayed for her. I planned to catch her if she fell.

I didn't realize it at the time but as I prayed for Alison, Terry Moore had walked up and placed his hand near my head praying for me.[1] I could feel a very strong presence of the Lord and a pressure coming from behind my head.

Nan Bagby turned toward me and touched my left arm with two fingers. When she did it felt like fire spread slowly up my arm and when it reached my shoulder, spread to all parts of my body. Everything went numb and tingly and I started to fall. I didn't fall because someone pushed me down. I fell because none of the muscles I normally use to stand were still responding. And even though it made a very loud noise when I hit the floor, it actually didn't hurt at all.

I landed flat on my back without being able to do anything to slow down the fall. Immediately, I tried to move and get up but the only muscles working were in a couple of my fingers, and I was having a hard time forming words. Nan

Bagby looked down at me and laughed and said, "You're not going anywhere. Just lay there and enjoy it."

A point of clarification I want to make here: Since then, any time I have fallen in the Spirit was because I was so numb I couldn't stand, and I would submit to what Holy Spirit was doing. I've never allowed anyone to push me down. By an act of faith I can submit to His will and be blessed.

> For the word of the cross is foolishness to those who are perishing, but to us who are being saved it is the power of God. [19] For it is written,
> "I will destroy the wisdom of the wise,
> And the cleverness of the clever I will set aside."
> [20] Where is the wise man? Where is the scribe? Where is the debater of this age? Has not God made foolish the wisdom of the world? [21] For since in the wisdom of God the world through its wisdom did not come to know God, God was well-pleased through the foolishness of the message preached to save those who believe.
>
> 1 Corinthians 1:18-21

Over time, I have tested the manifestations to see if I tried if could I stop any of them. The answer is yes. In most cases Holy Spirit requires a yielding to Him in order for Him to accomplish whatever He is doing at the time. By an act of my will I can stop the ministry or manifestation if I try.

Condensed Milk

Someone asked, "Why does God do this?" I have prayed for thousands of people and I've seen God heal people physically, but predominantly He reaches deep inside their heart and heals emotional wounds. It seems to me that this process the Lord uses is like when a physician puts a patient under anesthesia before performing surgery. Interestingly though, I've noticed more than one person the second they go out in the Spirit, they have rapid eye movement (REM). From what I understand, you're only supposed to be able to do that when you're asleep and you can't fake REM.

Often while praying for them I feel a silent cry coming out of them, and I know God is healing their heart and taking away pain. Sometimes as you pray, the Lord will tell you the source of their struggles. It could be an event that happened long ago.

Alison and I prayed for a lady in her sixties. She was struggling and had come up for prayer to determine if she and her husband should even continue in the ministry. We prayed for her and she fell out in the Spirit and coiled up into a fetal position and cried and cried. The Lord told me He was healing an emotional pain caused by an event that happened when she was five years old. I told her husband what the Lord had said and He told us when she was five, **her parents decided that they didn't want her anymore and put her up for adoption.**

The next day we saw the husband and looked around, but we didn't see his wife. When we started to talk to him, we realized she was standing right by him but we didn't recognize her, because she looked so beautiful, happy, younger and full of life. God had healed her heart so dramatically, she didn't look the same. God also had provided a financial miracle to save their ministry.

Falling out in the Spirit is ministry that God lets us participate in, but He's the One that's really doing all the work. It's really unique in that we have to submit to man and God at the same time, and it seems that He either heals our body or heals our heart or He speaks to us very clearly. We saw over and over again that in 15 to 45 minutes of "carpet time," the Lord would accomplish in minutes what would normally take months or years of counseling or therapy.

Condensed Milk

16. Laying on of Hands

Laying on of hands has always been fascinating to me. To me it's like when a master carpenter hands over his hammer to an apprentice. It's really God empowering us to do things in ministry only He can do.

> *These signs will accompany those who have believed: in My name they will cast out demons, they will speak with new tongues;* [18] *they will pick up serpents, and if they drink any deadly poison, it will not hurt them; they will lay hands on the sick, and they will recover."*
>
> *Mark 16:17-18*

In addition to people falling out in the Spirit by the laying on of hands, you can also lay on hands to heal the sick, to heal hearts, minds or emotions, even cast out demons.

You can also be filled with the Spirit through the laying on of hands.

> *Then they began laying their hands on them, and they were receiving the Holy Spirit.*
>
> *Acts 8:17*

By the Lord's leading, spiritual gifts can be imparted. In other words, a person who has a spiritual gift of tongues can impart it to another by faith through the laying on of hands. The gift is duplicated so that after the ministry is complete, both people have the gift. You can't impart a gift you don't have.

One time we got a sticky note with a friend's family member who needed prayer. We laid hands on the sticky note and felt a powerful release of the Lord's power. It was just as if they were there with us. By faith you can lay hands on and pray for someone who is not there physically.

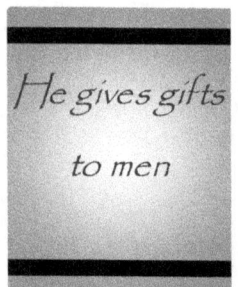

A couple of important points to know about praying for people, you can pray for someone without laying on of hands. You can also lay on hands without actually touching them. I usually don't touch the person but I try to hold my hand close to their head or heart as I feel the Lord lead. I pretty much don't touch women at all in ministry. I still minister to women, but I don't minister to them without my wife present.

Please note: **Just because you have received one or more spiritual gifts it isn't a merit badge** or any indicator of your level of spirituality. God gives gifts to His people for His purposes, not because we're more spiritual, holy or anything like that. I think sometimes He gives gifts to us just because we ask.

One evening we had been praying for people for hours. After I had prayed for the last one, I was walking through the congregation, a little drunk in the Spirit. I was loaded with anointing, more then I'd ever been. I walked up behind Linda Nicholas. She's an incredible woman of God. She was sitting on the floor praying for someone. I thought I even have enough anointing to take Linda out. She didn't see me as I placed my hand near the back of her head. But she felt the power of God and turned around and saw me.

She said, "No, you don't" and touched the toe of my shoe with two fingers.

My body was instantly overwhelmed by the power of God. I went straight down and hit the floor with a "bloof."

Good times, good times.

Condensed Milk

17. Resist Evil, Even Unto Death

It was a beautiful day. I was happy, driving to work, praying, and I asked the Lord, "Teach me something new. Teach me something I've never heard before."

He said, "Resist evil, even unto death."

I immediately crumbled and said, "What have I done now?"

He replied, "Why does it always have to be about you?"

Oh, I was so disappointed with myself. I said, "Oh Lord, I'm sorry. I apologize. Please forgive me. I'm listening now."

He said He had to resist evil when the Roman soldiers were whipping Him. He could've dropped them where they stood by an act of His will alone. I understood it to mean He could have killed them.

I told Him I recalled a hymn that said, "He could have called 10,000 angels …"

He said it was true; He could have called the angels.

But with great difficulty He had to resist killing the soldiers where they stood.

I said, "Where's that in the Bible?"

He replied, "Do you remember Ananias and Sapphira?"

I said, "I do. You are right. It's in the Bible, but Lord, even if You had taken their lives, wouldn't that have been justifiable homicide because You were innocent of any wrongdoing?"

He said, **"The evil that I had to resist even unto death was disobeying the command of the Father."**

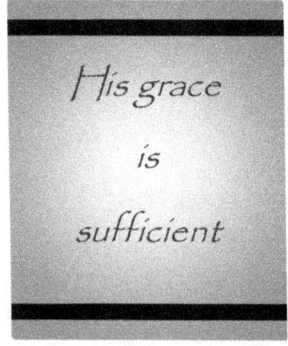

Taking their lives would have been a lack of submission to the will of the Father. Evil is the violation of God's purposes. It was the Father's will for Jesus to be crushed. It would have been evil for Jesus to interrupt His Father's plan even by stopping the torture.

Resist evil even unto death. Jesus did resist evil unto death, even death on a cross ...

> *But the Lord was pleased*
> *To crush Him, putting Him to grief;*
> *If He would render Himself as a guilt offering,*
> *He will see His offspring,*
> *He will prolong His days,*
>
> Isaiah 53:10

Surely our griefs He Himself bore,
And our sorrows He carried;
Yet we ourselves esteemed Him stricken,
Smitten of God, and afflicted.
⁵ But He was pierced through for our transgressions,
He was crushed for our iniquities;
The chastening for our well-being fell upon Him,
And by His scourging we are healed.
⁶ All of us like sheep have gone astray,
Each of us has turned to his own way;
But the Lord has caused the iniquity of us all
To fall on Him.

Isaiah 53:4-6

I complain to God when I have a bad day at work. Jesus didn't; He didn't complain. He submitted to the will of His Father; He trusted and He obeyed.

John testified about Him and cried out, saying, "This was He of whom I said, 'He who comes after me has a higher rank than I, for He existed before me.'" ¹⁶ For of His fullness we have all received, and grace upon grace. ¹⁷ For the Law was given through Moses; grace and truth were realized through Jesus Christ.

John 1:15-17

Grace upon grace

Grace and truth were realized through Jesus Christ. Grace is the game changer. Without grace we would never measure up to the requirements of the law. The law condemns but grace forgives. The law brings death but grace brings life. For by grace we can be saved through faith.

Jesus' next point, the real point of His teaching, went right over my head. But as best I understand, it's this: When Jesus resisted evil even unto death by obeying His Father, He gained grace that He is able to extend to us to help us resist evil and even cover our sin when we don't resist. His grace empowers us to be successful at whatever He leads us to do. And if we mess up, grace covers that, too.

Several weeks later, I was praying. Jesus indicated that all He overcame while here on earth has been credited to His account - grace that He can extend to us as needed for other situations.

> *Therefore let us draw near with confidence to the throne of grace, so that we may receive mercy and find grace to help in time of need.*
>
> *Hebrews 4:16*

18. The Daisy Bucket Anointing

One night very late after the Toronto revival meetings, there were a few of the ministers still there and a few dozen people still around. I had been sitting on the stage praying. There was such a strong presence of the Lord, and I heard God say, "You guys need to lighten up!"

I got up and was getting ready to leave when one of the guys on their ministry team asked, "Have you heard about the Daisy Bucket anointing?" The other guy ministering there said, "No, not the Daisy Bucket anointing! People are modeling what we're doing all over the world. Don't tell them about the Daisy Bucket anointing!"

We said, "No, we haven't. We haven't heard. What is it?" They went over and picked up this small one gallon bucket. It was a white plastic paint bucket from a local hardware store with daisies on the side of it, and they had stacks and stacks of them. They used them for taking the offering.

One of the guys grabbed a bucket and drew it along the floor on the carpet as if he was scooping up something like water. Then he went over to a girl sitting cross-legged on the floor looking toward heaven with her eyes closed and her back to him. He took the invisible contents of the Daisy

Bucket and poured it slowly over her head. She immediately started shaking and fell out in the Spirit without even opening her eyes. She was never aware that he was there or had done anything. And the guys were beside themselves laughing.

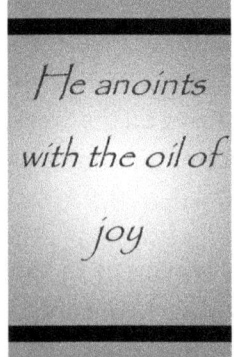

Then one of them said, "Check this out." And they scooped up some more anointing off the floor and then with a swishing or throwing action, threw the contents of the bucket through the air toward another person who had their back to them. Same as the first one, this person didn't see it coming and was immediately impacted when the invisible fluid reached him or her.

We were all laughing at this point. It was incredible and amazing but somehow tangible the way the Lord was ministering. The guys immediately started scooping up anointing and splashing each other. So drunk in the Spirit they became, they could hardly stand up, and they were laughing uncontrollably.

Alison was watching all of this, standing there with her purse, both of our Bibles, two water bottles, some videos she had bought with all of it stacked up in her arms. She was tired and ready to leave.

The Daisy Bucket Anointing

The guys both scooped up some more anointing from the floor and giggling and laughing, one of them said, "Watch this." He looked at Alison, and she said, "Oh, no, not me." Laughing, she started running down the aisle trying to get away.

He let her get quite a distance away and leaned back and made a throwing motion like he was throwing water out of the bucket toward her. Just as if it had been water and just as long as it would take it to travel through the air - the couple of seconds to reach her - when the anointing hit her, she was knocked up into the air and fell tumbling to the ground.

Purse, Bibles, videotapes and everything went flying in all directions. She fell out in the Spirit laughing, unharmed. Incredible! **God has such a sense of humor.**

I would hate to write a theological thesis on this one.

This is also a little out there too, much like sticking pennies to the wall. I like being out there though. I want to live on the edge of what God's doing, with my toes dangling over the cliff.

Alison and I have experienced the anointing on the floor several times over the years at different places. I would have to add humorously, we haven't scooped it up and thrown it around though.

Condensed Milk

We're created in God's image, and our God has a sense of humor. Most people imagine God as somewhat stoic. I think this story is an example of how God loves to play with His children. We do need to lighten up, trust God and reduce the stress in our life.

We also need to be careful not to put God in a box, like we know everything He can and will do.

19. Revival, Laughter

Spirit-led revivals are not the traditional path to spiritual growth but necessary for fast growth in these last days. Like mother's milk, we need revival less as we mature.

Before I was spirit-filled, I had little compassion. If I knew something bad happened to someone, I could barely dig any compassion out of my heart. I did care, but I wanted to care more - it just wasn't there. But God gave the tin man a heart, and after the refreshing revival, I cried all the time. Almost anything good or bad made me tear up.

When the Holy laughter hit our group they would come get me and all pray for me to receive the laughter, but I would just cry. It was almost like the Lord took us back to being children to work through the hurts we amassed when we were young.

It was a special time in our life. There were those who "caught the fire." They embraced the revival, probably because they were the most needy, hungry or brokenhearted. We played in the gifts of the Spirit and we grew fast in our understanding and knowledge. There were those who believed but didn't experience much or anything at all.

Then there were those who wanted the experience but for whatever reason they didn't experience anything. Many of those became bitter and said this was all demonic, that Holy Spirit would never have you do anything weird. They would say, "These ministers just play on your emotions and wind up the crowd." They quoted:

> *But all things must be done properly and in an orderly manner.*
>
> 1 Corinthians 14:40

In context this verse was referring to prophecy and tongues. None the less the church was divided over this move of the Spirit. I, for one, was changed forever. I wish everyone could just taste and see, press in and experience the life-changing power of Holy Spirit.

> *O taste and see that the Lord is good; How blessed is the man who takes refuge in Him!*
>
> Psalm 34:8

You don't have to experience the power of the Lord to be saved. But you don't have to wait until heaven, either, to experience some of the joys we'll know more fully there. Just ask the Lord to show you the Kingdom of God and His power. It takes more faith to believe in the things of God if you've never experienced His power.

I remember when I came to know the Lord. I wanted to tell everyone about Jesus. I wanted everyone I loved to have what I had. According to a book of the world's religions, I'm a third wave Pentecostal, and I want everyone I love to have what I have. If in reading this you think I'm lying or crazy, just ask the Lord. I trust Him to show you the truth.

> So Jesus was saying to those Jews who had believed Him, "If you continue in My word, then you are truly disciples of Mine; [32] and you will know the truth, and the truth will make you free."
>
> John 8:31-32

On a road trip I stopped at a rest stop on the Texas-Oklahoma border. I met the Reverend Charles and Irene Davis of Mission, Texas. He had been at the Catch the Fire Conference. He called it the "Laughing Revival" and told his wife, 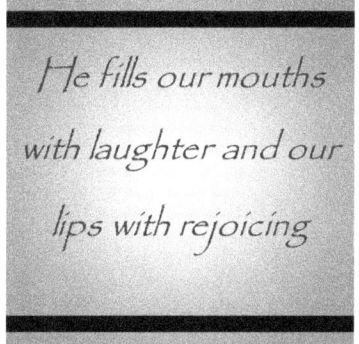 "Here's a Baptist boy been filled with the Holy Ghost, caught the fire and can't stand himself." Reverend Charles was part of the Latter Rain movement in the 40s. He believes this move of the Spirit is the final push before the Lord comes.

They called them followers of Jesus back in the day not just because they followed His teaching but also because they physically followed Him around.

Condensed Milk

Do the same - **be a follower of God!** Seek to find out where He is moving and what He's doing and go there.

The internet is a great tool. Use it to find out what God is doing in your community. Ask your friends who go to meetings and conferences at other churches. Look at the ministry calendars at churches in your area. Some churches will bring in special speakers and teachers from out of town for meetings and conferences. Or travel to Kansas City to the International House of Prayer (ihop.org) or Bethel Church in Redmond, California (ibethel.org). There are all kinds of great resources out there.

Pray and ask the Lord what He wants you to do. It's not too late to "Catch the Fire" and experience the joy of the "Laughing Revival."

Where He leads, I will follow.

20. The Halloween Bible

One Halloween our children decided they didn't want to celebrate Halloween but they didn't want to stay in the house with the lights turned off either. They asked if we could go to the Christian bookstore and buy some things to hand out for Halloween. We bought some pencils with Scripture on them but mostly got a bunch of those little New Testament Bibles.

On Halloween night, when the neighborhood children came and rang the doorbell, we handed out Bibles. The children and parents responded nicely. It certainly was a unique treat or gift.

Quite a long time later, maybe a year, we were driving through our neighborhood and saw a large book lying in the street. We stopped and picked it up - a nice, new Study Bible. We found a name and a phone number in it. We called the lady, and she came to our house to pick it up.

She rang the doorbell, and we opened the door. She had a very surprised look on her face as she told us who she was and that she was here to retrieve her Bible. She had driven off with it still on the car on her way to church and was glad we had found it.

Condensed Milk

We gave her the Bible, and she started to tear up and said, "You're the ones that gave out the New Testaments on Halloween."

We said, "Yes, we are."

She said she had taken the New Testament and started to read it. Then she started going to church and ... as she choked back the tears, she said, **"I'm a Christian now.** Thanks for giving out Bibles on Halloween."

Isn't God good?

This is the day which the Lord has made;
Let us rejoice and be glad in it.

Psalm 118:24

This made a huge impact on us. Had we stayed home with the porch light off or gone to a church-sponsored "Harvest Festival," we would've missed a wonderful opportunity.

We've been all over the map with this one, but we have decided that the Lord has given each day to us. We shouldn't hide and try to ignore secular holidays. Our Lord is a redeemer, and we should partner with God to do His will every day. Let's celebrate Jesus every holiday - and every day - and express His love and acceptance.

21. The Seven Tests of Man

A few years ago I met an incredible man of God named Jim O'Keefe, who has now gone on to be with the Lord. He told me that God had him go through seven tests. They were:

1. Fear of Man
2. Three Days in the Grave
3. Desert or Wilderness
4. Die to Self
5. Mammon or Money
6. Obedience
7. Fearing God

It's very possible these are not all the tests. I know He customizes each test for the individual.

> *The refining pot is for silver and the furnace for gold,*
> *But the Lord tests hearts.*
>
> *Proverbs 17:3*

The Lord will take us through the tests as part of the process He uses in training us to become what He created us to be.

Condensed Milk

During a test I assume a person must do or accept something they don't want. It seems to be an intense time of pressure or crushing where God changes your heart, your ways and your direction.

I don't think the Lord has a particular order you go through the tests. I've been through at least five of them, which includes the first and the last on the list. I'm not sure I've been through all of them. For that reason I don't have a teaching for each of the tests. I'm sure I haven't passed them all. The Word doesn't address them much other than the tests exist.

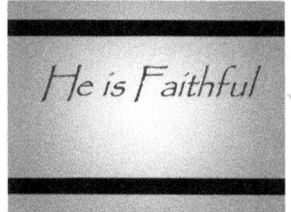

The Lord told me the purpose of the test is not for Him to know if I can pass the test (He already knows) but for me to know. I've also heard there's no need to worry if you don't pass a test; you get to take it over and over until you do.

> *You shall remember all the way which the Lord your God has led you in the wilderness these forty years, that He might humble you, testing you, to know what was in your heart, whether you would keep His commandments or not.*
>
> *Deuteronomy 8:2*

Don't let anyone sugarcoat this. The tests are hard - hands-down some of the hardest experiences of my life. Some of the tests are about trust - trusting God instead of ourselves. Some are about choices - to pass His test you must choose Him first. Some are about obedience - if you're sure it's God and it's not contrary to Scripture, just do it.

Blessed is a man who perseveres under trial; for once he has been approved, he will receive the crown of life which the Lord has promised to those who love Him.

James 1:12

At least for me I would say the "Fear of God" test impacted me the most. Maybe that was because God brought down my naive Pollyanna view of the world.

"Three Days in the Grave" was the first and hardest test the Lord put me through. For me it was three actual days, as it was for Jesus, Jonah and Paul. Jesus was in the grave (Matthew 12:40). Jonah was in a whale (Jonah 1:17). And Paul (Saul) was blinded (Acts 9:9). There's definitely a pattern here.

I won't discuss the details of my test, but from what I understand people experiencing sudden loss or separation from a loved one may be taking this test.

The Lord told me the tests are a witness of the faithfulness of God written on our hearts and minds in indelible ink as a testimony.

> *Beloved, do not be surprised at the fiery ordeal among you, which comes upon you for your testing, as though some strange thing were happening to you; ¹³ but to the degree that you share the sufferings of Christ, keep on rejoicing, so that also at the revelation of His glory you may rejoice with exultation.*
>
> 1 Peter 4:12-13

Trust God. He won't give you more than you can bear. He will be right there with you all the way.

22. Fear of Man

We had a contractor working in our office. He hadn't been in the computer field very long. Previously he'd been a police officer and mentioned that in his time as an officer, they'd threatened to take his gun away to keep him from shooting people and had taken his car away because he'd used it as a weapon. I would describe him as a contentious, angry man. He wasn't very skilled at his job.

The guys on my team became frustrated with him and started giving him work that didn't need to be done just to keep him busy. He was very threatening and bragged how he used to kill people when he was in the military. He told us multiple times that if we ever crossed him, he would kill us. **He explained in great detail how and where he would shoot us with a sniper rifle** from on top of the building next door. He said there was nothing anyone could do to stop him and there was no way anyone could prove he did it.

His poor attitude escalated into a yelling and cursing confrontation. Since I was in charge of managing the contract, it fell to me to decide whether or not we would keep him or terminate his contract. His company made it clear: If we terminated his contract, they would release him from their employment, as well.

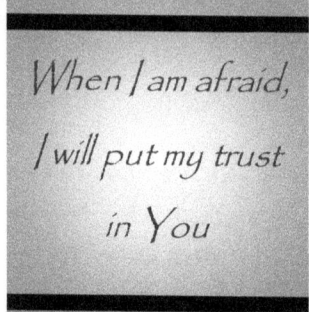

I thought about it and prayed about it. The only reason that I could find for not terminating his contract was - I was afraid of him. So was everyone else on the team. I decided I just needed to do the right thing because it was the right thing.

I called his company and let him go. He called my boss and begged for his job back. My boss told him the final decision was up to me and recommended that he call and apologize to me. Maybe I would give him his job back. (And if I didn't give him his job back, there was good chance it could cost me my life, maybe even the life of my family).

It seems far away now, but I spent all night awake in prayer and anguish as I struggled to seek the Lord, to determine His will, to make the right decision. I kept coming back to this: I needed to do the right thing because it was the right thing. I needed to trust God.

> The fear of man brings a snare, But he who trusts in the Lord will be exalted.
>
> Proverbs 29:25

Finally I received a phone call from him. He proceeded with a sincere apology. It came down to the fact that he wasn't skilled enough to do the work and had issues with getting along with others. I thanked him for his apology, but told him I was not going to give him his job back.

The next day I went to work and ended up working quite late. It was probably about ten o'clock at night when I left the building. I was the last person in the office to leave. As I walked out of the office, I looked over to the roof of the building next door. My heart was pounding. It was too dark to see anyone.

As I walked into the parking garage, I could see my car all the way at the end. To my right I could still see the top of the building next door where he said he would be perched. **The most terrifying moment was when I noticed that the only other car in the parking garage was the one parked next to mine - his red pickup truck.** I had a couple hundred feet to cross, out in the open and in full view of the building next door. It seemed like a hundred miles. The anxiety and the fear in me was over the top. I wondered what it would feel like to be shot.

I started to pray. The Lord said to me very clearly, **"Are you going to fear man or trust Me?"** I said, "I'm going to trust You, Lord." Each step I would say it over and over. It was a long walk. I didn't run; I just walked normally. As I walked, I looked around. I didn't see him. I got to my car and looked over. He wasn't in his truck. I unlocked my door, started the car, put it in reverse and drove home. I never saw him. I didn't see or hear from him for years.

Much later I saw him at a convention. He stopped and greeted me. He asked what I was doing and told me where he was working. It was like running into an old friend. I told myself, "A person who makes that many enemies, you just get lost in the wash."

> The Lord is my light and my salvation;
> Whom shall I fear?
> The Lord is the defense of my life;
> Whom shall I dread?
> ² When evildoers came upon me to devour my flesh,
> My adversaries and my enemies, they stumbled and fell.
> ³ Though a host encamp against me,
> My heart will not fear;
> Though war arise against me,
> In spite of this I shall be confident.
>
> Psalm 27:1-3

The fear of man isn't just about fearing the man with the gun. It could be fearing a boss, coworker, neighbor, spouse or relative.

The Lord won't necessarily deliver you every time. Look at Stephen. He trusted God, and they still stoned him. But there was no fear.

What it really comes down to is: Are we willing to trust the Lord?

> *Wait for the Lord; Be strong and let your heart take courage; Yes, wait for the Lord.*
>
> *Psalm 27:14*

The Lord can give us the ability to overcome fear with courage. It's really a matter of meditating and getting into your mind and your spirit what are the limits of what man can do to me compared to the vastness of God's mercy and loving-kindness, His capacity to keep us, to protect us. How big and powerful is what you fear, and how big and powerful is our God?

He can be trusted. **No Fear!**

> *In God I have put my trust, I shall not be afraid. What can man do to me?*
>
> *Psalm 56:11*

Condensed Milk

23. The Fear of the Lord

I was asking the Lord one day: If there are levels of Christian spiritual growth, what's the highest level? Is it like when your shadow touches someone and they're healed? Or is it when you can walk on water, etc.?

The Lord told me **the highest spiritual level was when someone truly fears the Lord.**

I was sitting on the porch swing the other day, meditating on this and talking to the Lord. I was trying to find out what I needed to do to grow spiritually enough to be where I feared Him. As I sat there I searched my heart and tried to find if there was any part of me that feared God. All I could find in my heart was the love that I had for Him - but no fear.

The next thing the Lord did was to reference a conversation we had back when I was first saved. Years ago the Lord had showed me in a vision all of the turning points - the points in a person's life where you make decisions that change the course of your life forever. Most of these decisions involve educational, relational, location, vocational, and spiritual choices.

I had made some bad decisions. I asked the Lord if He could send me back in time so I could correct the mistakes and make things right, so I could have a good life.

He told me no. He said if I could go back and change those events, then the world would have me and the world would be using the talents He gave me for its glory. He said, "But I have hidden you away." (I saw a vision of myself in His hand and He closed His fingers over me, to hide me.) He continued to say, "I will use the talents I gave you, for my glory, in my time."

Back to the present... **the Lord told me that He establishes the steps of a man, that it was He who set in motion the events that had ruined my life.**

I was shocked! How could this be so? He said, "You know it's true; you've even taught this."

We know when we walk through the valley of the shadow of death we will fear no evil for the Lord is there with us. He doesn't say He will take us out of the valley, or will make it go away, or even make it pleasant. **But who created the valley in the first place** (Psalm 23:4)?

It's still important that we go through it, and we'll be better for it. What about all the great men and women of God that you know and have read about? Every single one of them went through some difficult times to get them where God needed them to be.

...For he has torn us, but he will heal us; he has wounded us, but he will bandage us. ² He will revive us after two days; he will raise us up on the third day, that we may live before him.

Hosea 6:1-2

He pointed out in Scripture that He gave Joseph the dream that set in motion the difficult events that set the course of Joseph's life. It's in the Bible everywhere, but I just didn't see it.

Who threw Job under the bus? It was God who said to Satan, "Have you considered My servant Job? For there is no one like Him on the earth, a blameless and upright man, fearing God and turning away from evil." The Lord set all that followed in motion (Job 1:8).

How was the trip up the mountain for Abraham and Isaac? It took three days for them to get there. Abraham thought God wanted him to sacrifice his son and he was obedient to the end; that had to be tough.

I knew God allowed bad things to happen to us to grow us. **I didn't realize sometimes He caused them.** The revelation was harsh. I was crushed, then angry at Him. I refused to talk to Him for almost a week. Then I forgave Him, and asked Him to forgive me. He said He already had.

See, we Christians keep saying that the Lord is good. We even have a song that says the Lord is good all the time, but the world judges God and isn't sure God's good all the time. They know that bad things happen and they know enough about God to know that He could have prevented them. The world says why do the innocent suffer and die? Why do good things happen to bad people and bad things happen to good people? They know it's not fair, they know it's not right, and **quite frankly the Christian's answer has been pretty simplistic and naive.**

> He is King of Kings and Lord of Lords

He taught this to us plainly with Lazarus, but we didn't see it. We say sin, free choice and Satan are the source of all bad things in the world. Who created all of that? Who is powerful enough to stop it at any time?

No, it's clear to me His purpose in perfecting me is good. His methods can be harsh. Am I judging God? Probably, but I shouldn't be. I know His ways are higher than my ways and His thoughts are greater than mine.

He is willing to do whatever is necessary to bring me to where He wants me to be. We need to grasp the sovereignty of God. Who created who? And for whose purposes were we created? Are we not God's servants? We treat Him like He's our servant. We were made by Him, for Him, not the other way around. We pray and demand all good things to be poured out of heaven on us. But aren't the very best things He can do for us not always pleasant? He is directing our lives. He is a master composer and conductor directing our lives as part of His great symphony.

> *The mind of man plans his way,*
> *But the Lord directs his steps.*
>
> *Proverbs 16:9*

The Lord loves me so much that He's willing to cause me loss and/or pain to become what He wants me to be. He loves me so much that He was willing to sacrifice His Son to save me. He's willing to sacrifice me for the benefit of someone else.

But I must fear the Lord only, because only He has authority to bring or allow calamity in my life. There is none other to fear. No one else can do me harm without His permission. Look at Stephen - the Lord's sacrifice of Stephen was the highest point of Stephen's ministry, his crowning achievement.

So, do I fear God? Yes! I am beginning to fear Him. I'm afraid of what He'll do to perfect me. Or maybe more accurately, I'm afraid of the method He might choose to perfect me. The stakes are higher now. **This is not a game, and He's not playing.**

I reflect on what He's teaching me, and it makes me smile. I now know how committed He is to making me be who and what He created me for, how much more He must love us to do whatever must be done. We don't possess that much love for our own children.

Condensed Milk

You are Holy, Lord. Who have I but You, Lord? I must trust the Lord and His wisdom. The fear of the Lord is the beginning of wisdom; to depart from evil is understanding. We need to press in to know the Lord, to know the truth about the Lord and the truth shall set us free (Job 28:28).

You see, I wanted God to turn back time and correct my mistakes so I could have a "Good Life." But I needed those mistakes so I could gain the wisdom, faith and trust to have the good life He planned for me.

He promised He would never give me more than I could bear. There are times when we wonder how much more can we take. I've said more than once, "Lord, I can't take any more!"

He's made me stronger; I can bear more now. He has blessed me with endurance. And those dreams I had and the fear of an unknown future? Well, maybe I can trust Him now.

> *For I know the plans I have for you," declares the Lord, "plans to prosper you and not to harm you, plans to give you hope and a future.*
>
> *Jeremiah 29:11*

Hasn't He earned our trust? What more can He do, what more can He give? He is teaching us to trust Him even when we can't see Him. This is not just a random, meaningless existence - it's His plan, and it's working.

Bless our God, O peoples,
And sound His praise abroad,
[9] Who keeps us in life
And does not allow our feet to slip.
[10] For You have tried us, O God;
You have refined us as silver is refined.
[11] You brought us into the net;
You laid an oppressive burden upon our loins.
[12] You made men ride over our heads;
We went through fire and through water,
Yet You brought us out into a place of abundance.
[13] I shall come into Your house with burnt offerings;
I shall pay You my vows,
[14] Which my lips uttered
And my mouth spoke when I was in distress.
[15] I shall offer to You burnt offerings of fat beasts,
With the smoke of rams;
I shall make an offering of bulls with male goats.
Selah.
[16] Come and hear, all who fear God,
And I will tell of what He has done for my soul.

Psalm 66:8-16

The following is an old story from an unknown author. Silversmiths and the refining process are not commonplace. It is unlikely we would encounter them in our lives today. Our God is refining us and we need to understand that process.

Condensed Milk

Refining Silver

Some time ago, a few ladies met in a certain city to read the Scriptures and make them the subject of conversation. While reading the third chapter of Malachi they came upon a remarkable expression in the third verse: "And He shall sit as a refiner and purifier of silver." One lady's opinion was that it was intended to convey the view of the sanctifying influence of the grace of Christ. Then she proposed to visit a silversmith and report to them what he said on the subject.

She went accordingly and without telling the object of her errand, begged to know the process of refining silver, which he fully described to her. "But, Sir," she said, "Do you sit while the work of refining is going on?" "Oh, yes, Madam," replied the silversmith. "I must sit with my eye steadily fixed on the furnace, for if the time necessary for refining be exceeded in the slightest degree, the silver will be injured."

The lady at once saw the beauty, and comfort, too, of the expression, "He shall sit as a refiner and purifier of silver." Christ sees it needful to put His children into a furnace; His eye is steadily intent on the work of purifying, and His wisdom and love are both engaged in the best manner for them. Their trials do not come at random; "the very hairs of your head are all numbered."

As the lady was leaving the shop, the silversmith called her back and said he had forgotten to mention that the only way that he knows when the process of purifying is complete is when he sees his own image reflected in the silver ...

--Author Unknown

A few days later I was talking to the Lord and He asked, "Do you remember the refiner's fire?" I said, "Yes, I remember something about the purest gold having to be refined seven times." Humorously, He added, "You have to let the gold cool down between [refining's]."

So if you're in a quiet, peaceful time in your life, you may be in between the difficult times of refining. (We get a break from time to time.)

> In this you greatly rejoice, even though now for a little while, if necessary, you have been distressed by various trials, ⁷so that the proof of your faith, being more precious than gold which is perishable, even though tested by fire, may be found to result in praise and glory and honor at the revelation of Jesus Christ;
>
> 1 Peter 1:6-7

Terry Moore says, "Anything you can see, you can touch, is not your problem. If you can pinch it, then it's not the problem." It could be a demonic attack. Back to the example of Job, his was a demonic attack. The Lord set clear limits on what Satan was allowed to do and what he was not.

> Are not two sparrows sold for a cent? And yet not one of them will fall to the ground apart from your Father.
>
> Matthew 10:29

Condensed Milk

Charles Stanley says to view all adversity as coming from God, not from someone else.[1] Ask the Father, "What is your goal for my life in this adversity?" Surrender to the unknown will of God. You can rest in His trustworthiness to see you through this. The Lord can be trusted.

> *Consider it all joy, my brethren, when you encounter various trials, [3] knowing that the testing of your faith produces endurance.*
>
> *James 1:2-3*

No matter whose hand delivers the adversity - a boss, a co-worker, a family member or a friend - the Lord commands us to forgive. What damage we have inflicted! What a poor witness I have been! As they hated me, I hated them back. As I worked through it and prayed, I eventually forgave them. But is that what they saw at the time of the attack - the love of God, unconditional forgiveness?

> *For if you forgive others for their transgressions, your heavenly Father will also forgive you. [15] But if you do not forgive others, then your Father will not forgive your transgressions.*
>
> *Matthew 6:14-15*

Chuck Swindoll says, "When a person goes through a difficult time, they either get bitter or better."

God didn't keep Shadrach, Meshach and Abednego out of the fire, but He was with them through it. They didn't focus any anger or blame toward Nebuchadnezzar. So God used this to grow the three of them and to witness to the king.

> *I have been crucified with Christ; and it is no longer I who live, but Christ lives in me; and the life which I now live in the flesh I live by faith in the Son of God, who loved me and gave Himself up for me.*
>
> Galatians 2:20

Is this the message of the cross? I must die to self and trust God. We are not able to grasp an infinite God. God's ways and His plans are sometimes difficult for us to comprehend. He leads us into impossible situations where our only option is to trust Him. In trusting Him, He grows our faith.

> *But he said to her, "You speak as one of the foolish women speaks. Shall we indeed accept good from God and not accept adversity?" In all this Job did not sin with his lips.*
>
> Job 2:10

The fear of the Lord - it's there, it's in your face. I just didn't want to believe it's true.

> *But whatever things were gain to me, those things I have counted as loss for the sake of Christ. [8] More than that, I count all things to be loss in view of the surpassing value of knowing Christ Jesus my Lord, for whom I have suffered the loss of all things, and count*

them but rubbish so that I may gain Christ, ⁹ and may be found in Him, not having a righteousness of my own derived from the Law, but that which is through faith in Christ, the righteousness which comes from God on the basis of faith,

Philippians 3:7-9

If God is good, then why does He allow the innocent to suffer and die?

First of all, there is no one who is innocent. We were all born into sin.

Secondly, He does it out of His great purpose and divine love and wisdom for our good or for our discipline, so we can grow and learn to trust Him.

Last point: there are many who translate fear of God into awe of God. We should be in awe of God and we should be reverent. Yet in both the Greek and the Hebrew the same word translated *fear* as in "fear of God" is also translated as fear in "do not *fear,*" "should I *fear* in days of adversity" and "what the wicked *fears.*" This is why they didn't translate these as "do not *awe,*" "should I *awe* in days of adversity" and "what the wicked *awes.*"

We may not like the concept of fearing God, but it is a concept He wants us to grasp.

So the church throughout all Judea and Galilee and Samaria enjoyed peace, being built up; and going on

> in the fear of the Lord and in the comfort of the Holy Spirit, it continued to increase.
>
> Acts 9:31

The Lord told me:

"The Red Sea.
I put that sea there.
When I created it, I knew someday
it would be an impervious barrier
that would mean certain death to my people.
I parted that sea,
to increase the faith of my people.
I brought down those walls of water
to keep the world from following them
into my blessing."

What is impossible for man is possible for God.

God knew when He created the Red Sea that in the future it would be a barrier to His people fleeing from Pharaoh causing extreme adversity. He also knew He would use it to perform an extreme faith-building miracle. Then He would use it again to keep Pharaoh's army from threating them anymore.

> *The fear of the Lord leads to life,*
> *So that one may sleep satisfied, untouched by evil.*
>
> Proverbs 19:23

Condensed Milk

To wrap this up, often we seek God in adversity, grow closer to Him, or the adversity results in greater good. What is the fear of the Lord? It's not dreading what He will do, but trusting Him to do what's best for me, my family and friends even if it requires want or suffering. It's embracing the pain. If I think God isn't in control, I can just rail at my misfortune. But if I trust God, then I know He's in this for my good and I'm never alone. He will stick through this with me. Even if this time ends in death, I will purpose to trust Him and His wisdom because I know His plan is for the greater good.

> *The Lord is my light and my salvation;*
> *Whom shall I fear?*
> *The Lord is the defense of my life;*
> *Whom shall I dread?*
>
> Psalm 27:1

When I first read Psalm 27, I understood it to mean I don't need to fear anyone anymore. Now after reading this psalm almost every day for more than a year, I finally get it. **He is the only one to fear.** My God is in control of my life and my world. He is willing to do whatever it takes to grow me to where He needs me to be. He is in control - so much so that no one and nothing can touch me without His permission. I belong to Him.

Whom shall I fear? The Lord is the only One to fear.

There is no one else to fear but God.

24. You Can't Out Give God

Learning to Tithe

A couple of years after Alison and I were married, we started attending church regularly again for the first time since we were teenagers. We felt like the Lord wanted us to start tithing and to give a particular amount. The amount wasn't anywhere close to 10 percent. We did the math and determined if we didn't eat or buy gas, we could make it. We gave anyway.

The next few days, unusual checks began to arrive in the mail. The phone company reimbursed our deposit. A doctor's office refunded an overpayment. Mom sent us a random twenty. Almost all of them odd dollars and cents, like however many dollars and 63 cents.

After two weeks and over a dozen checks, I laughed and asked Alison if any more money had arrived with the mail that day. When we opened the mail box there was yet another random check.

At this point we both knew this was beyond coincidence. I asked her if she had kept a record of all the checks. She had recorded the deposits in her check register. When we added them up the balance was an even dollar amount (no cents). It was exactly five times (to the penny) what we had given to the church for a tithe.

This was a big step for us - for it was about obedience and trusting God, a living interactive God, who won't ask you to do something impossible and leave you hanging. This was also one of our first miracles. You can read about the feeding of the five thousand, but it's a whole different ballgame when you've been fed. It's much more exciting to receive provision from God than to provide for yourself.

Last but not least was the realization that the King of Kings and Lord of Lords cared enough about us individually - not just the collective church - that He would deliberately bless us in such a way that we couldn't deny from whom the blessing came. The Lord's attention to detail is astounding. You can never out give God.

> Honor the Lord from your wealth
> And from the first of all your produce;
>
> Proverbs 3:9

A Radio, a Car and a Washing Machine

I was driving to work one day in my Volkswagen Jetta, trying to listen to some Christian teaching. My car radio had issues. The on-off switch no longer worked so I had wired in a new one. The volume control no longer worked so you had to pound on the dash to adjust the volume. When you hit a bump, it would also change.

I had been pounding the dash for a while (to adjust the volume) when I prayed and asked the Lord if I could have a new radio. Then I thought about how many more pressing needs my family had and I stopped short and asked Him to forget that request and please forgive me for asking. See, we only had one car and Alison and I had to share it. That week our old, used washing machine had died. I was pretty good at fixing it but a lot of parts and fluids had come out the bottom - beyond a cost-effective repair.

We went shopping and Alison looked at dozens of machines and picked out the one she wanted with all the right features for our growing family. It was 500 dollars. We didn't have the money.

A few days later I walked out the door to go to work and a policeman was standing beside my car in front of our house taking notes. When I reached my car there was broken glass everywhere. I noticed through the broken window an ugly hole where my radio had been. He told me a guy in a brand new Cadillac was driving through the neighborhood stealing radios out of German cars. I told the officer my radio didn't work, and if they caught the guy, don't bother bringing it back.

I spoke to the insurance agent. I also told him my stolen radio didn't work. He said he understood and appreciated my honesty, but they could only replace it with a new one. I ended up with a much better radio than the one I had. The dash was damaged and since the car wasn't new anymore, rather than replacing, they repaired it. I called my insurance agent and he said that was okay with him and if there was any money left over we could keep it. That left us with $500.

Alison's father called that night, and said he went to buy a new car and they offered him $500 trade-in for his old one. I said I would give him $500, so he sold us his car. A few weeks later on Christmas Day we were opening presents when we opened a gift envelope. It contained the pickup receipt for a brand new washing machine - the exact one Alison had picked out!

It seems her Mom and Dad decided they should have given the car to us. They took the money we gave them and went out and bought a washing machine for us, not knowing which one Alison had picked out.

God had provided us with a brand new radio, a car (a '67 Chevy Malibu) and a brand new washing machine, and it didn't cost us one thin dime!

A Conference Call

God speaks through people. We had our largest financial decision before us. Conventional wisdom would recommend borrowing. We didn't feel like the Lord wanted us to. We went to a church conference the day before we had to decide. The speaker was from out-of-state and didn't know us or anything about the decision we faced.

In the middle of a teaching session the speaker stopped teaching, turned around and said to us, "The Lord is more than capable of taking care of the needs of you and your little family." We laughed. I thought to myself, well that means not to borrow, or then again it could mean it's okay to borrow.

Suddenly once again the speaker stopped and said, "The Lord God says don't borrow the money!" Clearly, our financial decision was much easier to make.

A Caribbean Cruise

Years ago, the Lord had started encouraging us to give more than a tithe. He told us the exact amount He wanted us to give, but we didn't know to where or for what. Within the next few weeks we heard of the church's construction project and after very little prayer knew that was where He wanted us to give.

Quite honestly, this was the first time in a long while we had experienced sacrificial giving. It was harder than I remembered. It didn't really require any faith at this point to know the Lord is more than capable of taking care of the needs of me and my little family, but I've grown accustomed to a few luxuries that might not make the cut.

In the early days I was so excited about just being used by God. Now I sometimes find myself struggling to be a

Condensed Milk

cheerful giver. Don't get me wrong. I love to give, but I prefer to give the extra money I don't really need.

We had been planning for over a year to give our daughters a surprise for Christmas - a Caribbean cruise. We planned to go during Spring Break. With the money we had already saved and what we could save by then, we could do this easily, we thought. We decided a few weeks before Christmas to go ahead and buy the tickets and gift wrap them. We went online to buy the tickets and were shocked to discover we couldn't afford them. We tried everything and every ship, every combination. Even if we could have stowed away on cots in the engine room, it wasn't going to work. No matter what we tried, we just didn't have enough money.

What had changed? It was the sacrificial giving. That may be why it's called "sacrificial." We had given ourselves right out of the cruise. The dream died, and I was devastated. I didn't even want to participate in our Christmas Day ritual of opening the presents. I tried to shake it off and then finally let it go.

Just before Spring Break we received an unexpected surprise from someone who didn't know anything about our failed plans. A Christian businessman I had done some work for was pleased with how I had resolved a difficult issue. So in addition to my wages he decided to bless my family with an all-expense-paid vacation.

The next week found us flying to Miami to board a ship named Imagination for a 5-day cruise to the Caymans and Jamaica with our daughters ... imagine that!

I don't know that this trip was a result of our giving. Maybe it was just a coincidence. That was the most expensive vacation we had ever had. To have failed plans resurrected at the last minute seems against all odds.

The Lord can be a lavish, extravagant giver. They say you can't out-give God. I hope this challenges your beliefs of what God can and will do. I hope this sets your expectations higher.

You know you could say that's great, but that was back then. What's God doing now - today? Well if you were to ask, if you could, I would have to say, somewhat embarrassingly, as I finished writing down this testimony, a check came in the mail, unexpected, in the amount totaling slightly more (by 10%) than the sum of all those checks in my first story. What a coincidence.

> Bring the whole tithe into the storehouse, so that there may be food in My house, and test Me now in this," says the Lord of hosts, "if I will not open for you the windows of heaven and pour out for you a blessing until it overflows.
>
> Malachi 3:10

Condensed Milk

25. The Wilderness

I was talking to the Lord the other day and made a passing remark about being in the desert. I felt I was being punished like when Moses had to live in the desert for 40 years. The Lord immediately corrected me. Moses was not being punished, he was being trained. He needed to learn the survival skills necessary to stay alive in the desert, so he could use those skills on his next job: Keeping the children of Israel alive in the desert for another 40 years.

Could it be that what we see as a negative "Wilderness Experience" is really a good thing? Paul apparently spent a lot of time with Jesus during his wilderness experience. The Lord shared with him some amazing teaching that Paul used in his next job (evangelizing Asia) and passed on to us in his letters (parts of the New Testament).

If you look at the lives of many great men of God, they seem to all go through a wilderness experience. The Lord doesn't seem to deliver us from the process but He does promise to go through it with us. And we'll be stronger for it. The wilderness can also be a time of testing - or in the case of Jesus - it ended with a satanic temptation.

Condensed Milk

> *Even though I walk through the valley of the shadow of death, I fear no evil, for You are with me;*
>
> Psalm 23:4

Many times I have complained to the Lord, "I don't want to do that" or "I don't want to have to learn that." From His perspective, He's educating me for the next assignment. Could it be this life is not about me and my plans? **Could it be this is about His plans, and "life" as we know it is just training for the next gig?**

Is it just me or does God put something inside us all that says I was created for a purpose, maybe for something special? But that special purpose hasn't happened yet and I'm wondering if it ever will. God tells me I won't be disappointed, but so far I am. I am amazed at what He's taught me though and how difficult it was to learn.

I think about all the saints I've known that were special to me but never really did anything amazing. They were so capable and had so much potential. One hundred and twenty years or less is not much time in light of eternity. Is this just school, maybe kindergarten? Are the amazing times yet to come?

I used to think life was just a story about the battle between good and evil. But it's not.

It's about His story. It has always been about Jesus Christ.

26. Rome Wasn't Built in a Day

I was working for a large company developing decision support software. In a meeting with the executives, we tried to define all of the elements we wanted to include in the software. At several points they asked for functionality that the technology couldn't do. I had to tell them "no" several times so when they asked for the ability to have an interactive hierarchal representation of their business units, I agreed to do it. I wasn't sure how I was going to accomplish it, but thought it shouldn't be that difficult.

Months later when it came down to actually writing the software, I wrote it several times. But even on the fastest computers it wasn't able to process all the information fast enough. Everything I tried, nothing worked. My last resort was to pray and ask God to help me out. God's a great programmer; He wrote DNA.

After a short prayer I sat down at the computer again and straight typed out an entire module. I compiled the program and was surprised that it worked the first time. Not only that, it was very fast and worked flawlessly. I named it "Roam" since you would use it to roam up and down the entity structure tree.

Some aspects of the program were beautiful in their simplicity, but other parts were ridiculously complex. At the core of this program was a four-dimensional array. To put that in layman's terms, I would say a two-dimensional array is like a spreadsheet with rows and columns. A three-dimensional array would be lots of pages of those spreadsheets put together. A four-dimensional array would be cubes of the three-dimensional arrays all associated together.

The point is: It's complicated. I spent the next two weeks going through the software and trying to understand exactly how it worked. But it was too complicated to understand.

I finished and installed the program with the "Roam" routine. Shortly after that, I got a job offer from a new company and left to work for them. My previous employer hired someone to maintain the software I had written. Several months later I got a phone call from him. He said he had been studying the program I wrote. He said it was well-written, well-documented and easy to understand. Except there was this one routine he had spent the last two weeks trying to understand. And although it worked perfectly, he had no idea how it worked. He said the routine was named Roam and asked what I knew about it.

I laughed and said, "Well, **Rome wasn't built in a day**." Instantly I had a check in my spirit. The Lord said, "Tell him the truth." I told him I had typed that module but probably didn't write it. I had typed it out in a few minutes after praying and asking God for help. I, too, had spent weeks studying it but was never able to figure it out.

There was an uneasy silence on the other end of the phone, and he quickly changed the subject. It was a rocky start, but over time we grew to be friends.

Several years later I got a panic call from him. He was having marital problems. He told me I was the only real Christian he knew and asked if we could meet. I met with him and after talking for some time, he asked where I attended church. I told him I was helping out at another church that was having a revival service that night and invited him to go. He showed up, went up for prayer, was radically saved, slain in the spirit, filled with the Spirit, and he's never been the same.

Now he's a changed man, a man of integrity who loves the Lord. All because of a miracle God did that you just wouldn't think He would do - writing a software program.

Don't think that God doesn't understand the work you do. He knows everything and is more than willing to help you in anything you do including your job.

Condensed Milk

I was having an arrogant, prideful moment in a meeting at work one day. We were meeting with a director of another division who had systems failing multiple times a day. He said this was normal and accused me of not being honest about my failure rates.

I became angry and slammed my fist down on the table and said emphatically, "My systems never fail!" In the embarrassing silence that followed I heard the Lord say, "You say your systems never fail. You're right. I've been bailing you out for years."

I've had a number of good ideas in my work that have really helped my career, but they probably weren't my ideas at all. God loves us so much He just gives good things all the time - without taking credit. He has told me many times, "You are successful because I make you successful."

There are people who believe that God limits Himself only to actions previously recorded in scripture. I haven't noticed any software-writing in the scriptures. It isn't like God said He'd love to help you but He can't find a scripture for that.

I have noticed He is God. He does what He wants, how He wants, when He wants, for our benefit. Our lack of faith and trust is often the most limiting factor.

For nothing will be impossible with God."

Luke 1:37

I need to be patient and trust God. I need to give Him the time He needs to grow me. I need to rest in knowing He knows what's best for me. I need to believe He's capable of completing what He's started.

I need to wait on the Lord, be strong and let my heart take courage.

Because after all ...

Rome wasn't built in a day.

Condensed Milk

27. Conversations with God

In talking with the Lord I heard Him say "I know" in response to my concerns. I asked Him, "How do you talk to a God who knows everything already?" He replied, "With practice."

> *pray without ceasing;*
>
> 1 Thessalonians 5:17

Someone once asked me why I don't pray out loud much. It's hard for me to pray out loud because I have to rehearse what's in my head to compose what I want to say. Then after you've rehearsed it in your head, you say it out loud. Since God can also hear our thoughts, He has already heard it several times and there's no point in saying anything. Therefore my lack of spontaneity causes my prayer to only benefit the other people listening in the room. My original intent to benefit God could easily turn into the prayer of the hypocrite and just be a point of pride (Mathew 6:5).

I'm not saying I'm opposed to or it's wrong to pray out loud. Clearly Jesus prayed aloud many times, and His prayers blessed those around Him. We also have been blessed by the spoken prayers of pastors, friends and others. I'm just saying, at least for me, it's hard to pray in spirit and in truth in such a manner that it blesses both God and man.

Last but not least, it's really annoying to the other people in the room who are waiting for their turn to pray when you stop to listen for anything that God may say. They can't differentiate between when I'm listening and when I'm done. Unless we all agree before the prayer that you can't take your turn unless the previous person says "Amen." That seems rather silly, though.

On the humorous side: Have you ever heard someone pray to God in Old English, "For thou wilt sayeth, thou kingdom cometh"? That just doesn't make sense to me. If God can understand hundreds of different languages then He can understand modern English.

The prayers that annoy me the most are the ones where they preach a sermon or deliver a reprimand out loud. You have to wonder if these prayers make it through the ceiling.

Most people pray in one direction, like a text or an email, although if you were to read the text of most of these prayers, it would be hard to distinguish whether they were intended to be sent to God or mailed to the North Pole. **Our God is not Santa Claus.**

What if we were to pray to God like a cell phone call? We need to treat God like He's a real person, like He's alive and actually listening to our prayers. Also, we need to stop to listen for a reply.

We tend to pray "our list" to God. If we have any questions at all, we tend to ask God questions without waiting for a response. We need to ask questions with expectation! We need to listen for and expect a response. And if you don't get an answer, ask again, and again and again. I think He likes our persistence.

I've asked the Lord thousands of questions. Thousands of times I've listened for a response and there was nothing but silence. Sometimes He would surprise me with a response, and then He was gone. I felt like shouting, "Wait! I have questions!"

He's training us to hear Him and to be sensitive to His leading. Most likely you've already experienced this. Have you ever been driving and felt a need to go on a different route than you normally do? Or experienced some unusual delay that slows you down and keeps you from being present at the scene of an accident or event that could've caused you harm? The Lord is training us to be sensitive to His leading.

Sometimes when I'm in a conversation with someone, the Lord will advise me quietly. He might say something like, "Don't say that." Or "Just be quiet and listen."

Condensed Milk

The Lord has shared with me some things that are pretty difficult to believe. Often, when sharing with people what the Lord has taught me, I tend to hold back. At that point in the conversation, almost always, I'll hear Him say, "Just tell them the truth." I'll think, "Lord, they can't handle this." To which He replies, "Tell them the truth, full disclosure."

> *God, after He spoke long ago to the fathers in the prophets in many portions and in many ways, [2] in these last days has spoken to us in His Son, whom He appointed heir of all things, through whom also He made the world.*
>
> *Hebrews 1:1-2*

When I stop to pray, my goal would be to quiet myself, press in and feel His presence. Wait for Him. Once connected, I would probably start off with, "Good morning, Lord. I love You. I praise You, and I worship You. Then I would pause and listen. I might continue with, "Thanks for spending time with me this morning. It's a beautiful day." I would listen for a response.

Recently I said, "I plan to study my Bible here in a few minutes." He said, "Daniel 9." To which I replied, "Daniel, Chapter 9 again? This is the third day in a row. Please help me understand what it is You want me to learn."

I usually bring up my top worries or concerns (like He didn't know or has forgotten). I might intercede and mention friends, family. I might say, "Please help Alison today. She's having a difficult time." I might close with, "I need to get with You at lunch. I love You, Lord. I worship You, Lord. I've gotta go." I usually throw in an "Amen."

We should be careful to pray every prayer acknowledging that God exists. He wants to have a relationship with us. We can pray "email style" to Him, and we can read the Word to get His response, but the relationship can be so much deeper.

Have you ever heard Him tell a joke? Funny, really funny. He will tell you things you have no way of knowing. He will tell what He loves about you, and it will break your heart.

> *Then you will call upon Me and come and pray to Me, and I will listen to you.*
>
> *Jeremiah 29:12*

I have to come clean in this chapter and confess sometimes I'm a whiner. Most of the time the Lord puts up with my whining. He has responded rather sternly a few times. I'm sure He prefers open honest dialog as opposed to a prefabricated, pretentious prayer.

I heard a story once of a new Christian using bad four-letter words in a prayer in church. The Lord said not to reprimand her; that was an honest expression of her heart. She didn't mean to be offensive.

If you don't take away anything else from this book, let me challenge you to deepen your prayer life. This part of my relationship with God is so meaningful and fulfilling to me

Condensed Milk

that I want everyone to have what I have. Maybe you already do. Even then I know I don't have nearly as deep a prayer life as Paul or Jesus had. But I can see from here how much better it could be.

We need to press in to know the Lord, to hear the Lord. Day or night, the King of Kings, the Lord of Lords is waiting for you. He will always make time for you - no matter how much time you need. He will be with you when you cry - you don't need to cry alone. He'll laugh with you, celebrate your victories and amaze you with His creative words and how He answers prayers.

You see, to Him you are priceless. And as hard as it is to believe, He wants to have a personal relationship with you. He wants to be closer to you than we are to ourselves. He lives in us and through us. We are what He does. Twenty four hours a day, seven days a week. He never sleeps.

You are a love of His life, and He's been waiting for you. He's not waiting there to judge you. He's waiting patiently for you - to love you, to help you. He's the One who really has your back. He's the One who will always be there for you. He's the One that makes a difference.

For you were created for love; you were created for worship. Our life is really not ours. It belongs to the One who gave Himself up for us, and we'll never really be happy unless we give ourselves back to Him.

28. Little Helicopters

One night Alison and I were praying for a couple. The Lord revealed to each of us individually some problems they had in their lives. The issues were overwhelming; I couldn't see how their marriage could survive. We weren't in a position to speak into their lives. I began to pray for the man. I was pressing Holy Spirit for how or what to pray for, when suddenly a wave of compassion came over me, and I felt in my heart more pain than I could bear. I had to stop praying for them.

That night I had a dream. In the dream the Lord lifted that man up from earth into the heavens. He was suspended in place, in time, like on an invisible timeline. The Lord could go backwards or forwards and look at any point in this man's life. Next He brought out the heart of the man and opened it. A myriad of little containers came from the heart and spread out to fill the expanse, all in neat little rows and columns but as countless as the stars of the sky.

I stretched out my arms to try to "put my arms around or grasp the situation." I directed all the capacity of my mind and spirit to understand how the pieces related to each other, but the weight of it all was more than I could bear - I thought it would crush me. I could sense the Lord's compassion at my failed attempt, as my motives were pure - I wanted to help.

> How precious also are Your thoughts to me, O God! How vast is the sum of them!
> ¹⁸ If I should count them, they would outnumber the sand.
> When I awake, I am still with You.
>
> *Psalm 139:17-18*

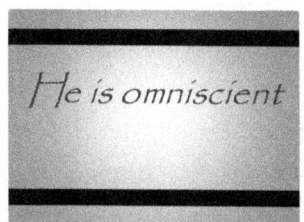

Next, we zoomed in on one of the little hovering containers. (It looked like a little helicopter to me.) The Lord showed me this particular container housed an unresolved issue, the consequences of a particular sin. The Lord took me closer to the hovering container. I was surprised to find up close they were quite large. I could see into an open cargo bay door in the side and saw a pallet sitting inside. The pallet contained a very large number of packages, records of all the information related to this one issue. I could see they were all numbered, counted and cataloged. I thought of the verses:

> He counts the number of the stars; He gives names to all of them. ⁵ Great is our Lord and abundant in strength; His understanding is infinite.
>
> *Psalm 147:4-5*

Indeed, the very hairs of your head are all numbered.

Luke 12:7

Although the Lord didn't show me the contents of any other container, most of them contained consequences of sin. Others were dreams, desires, virtues, relationships and beliefs - both good and bad.

It was unfathomable; the complexity of how they all related to each other was off the scale. **It made DNA look like Tinker Toys.** Finite man cannot grasp all the pieces. Holy Spirit was showing me that I simply don't have the capacity to really know the heart of any man - even my own heart.

Search me, O God, and know my heart;
Try me and know my anxious thoughts;
²⁴ And see if there be any hurtful way in me,
And lead me in the everlasting way.

Psalm 139:23-24

I had been pressing Holy Spirit to know the issues so I would know how to pray for them. After having this dream, I realized my only option was to trust the Lord. He knows what the issues are and what to do.

Maybe I should spend more time listening than hammering Him with requests and demanding that He do something when I don't understand all the issues. I need to seek His direction more. He is more than capable of revealing His will or giving directions on how to minister or what to do or say.

I want to be part of the solution and not part of the problem. I need to trust Him more, but most of all I need to not get my feelings hurt when the Lord does not respond when or how I want Him to.

> *O LORD, You have searched me and known me. [2] You know when I sit down and when I rise up; You understand my thoughts from afar. [3] You scrutinize my path and my lying down, and are intimately acquainted with all my ways. [4] Even before there is a word on my tongue, behold, O LORD, You know it all. [5] You have enclosed me behind and before, and laid Your hand upon me. [6] Such knowledge is too wonderful for me; it is too high, I cannot attain to it.*
>
> Psalm 139:1-6

> "For My thoughts are not your thoughts, nor are your ways My ways," declares the LORD. [9] "For as the heavens are higher than the earth, so are My ways higher than your ways and My thoughts than your thoughts."
>
> Isaiah 55:8-9

29. His Love

Have you ever noticed how when someone's born they're very self-centered and don't have much capacity for love? Most babies get showered with love. If they don't, it affects their emotional growth. It seems as we grow so does our need for love and our capacity to love. We go through phases where we are the center of our world. Some of us will love our parents, a girlfriend or boyfriend, our hobbies or careers. Even if we are satisfied for a while, we come back to an emptiness that needs something more.

People have come up with all kinds of wrong ways to fill the void, but they won't really satisfy. Only God can fill the void. The funny thing is as we grow in our love for Him, He gives us more capacity to love. We can love more people and the ones we already love we can now love much deeper.

God created us for Him. He saw our heart and said it's not good for man to be alone.

> *Then the Lord God said, "It is not good for the man to be alone; I will make him a helper suitable for him."*
>
> *Genesis 2:18*

Condensed Milk

He loved man so much He created woman. Man loved woman and woman loved man but they rebelled against God by doing what He told them not to. Today, so many people reject the Lord. He doesn't appear to love us any less.

How much love does it take to - if our spouse was lonely and we couldn't be with them, could we love our spouse so much that we would give them another because we knew they needed love they couldn't receive from us? How much love does that take? I can't even fathom that.

But God loves us that much. He created Adam for himself, and we are the bride of Christ. That's exactly what He did. He gave us away to someone else to satisfy the needs we weren't yet able to receive from Him. This is one of the most profound expressions of God's love for us.

> *And the man and his wife were both naked and were not ashamed.*
>
> *Genesis 2:25*

We can stand before our spouse naked and unashamed due to the depth of our relationship and because we love and trust them. Adam stood before the Lord naked and was unashamed. I couldn't do that. Is it because of sin? Or is it because I lack the relationship, love or trust? With me - it's probably the trust. I seem to always come up short in this area. Maybe I trust my wife more than the Lord.

Some people to this day don't love Him at all. Some people don't even acknowledge His existence. He loves us so much He came to earth and died on a cross to keep from losing us. I don't think we have the capacity to even begin to grasp the extravagant love He has for us. We would never doubt Him if we did.

> *Love is patient, love is kind and is not jealous; love does not brag and is not arrogant, ⁵ does not act unbecomingly; it does not seek its own, is not provoked, does not take into account a wrong suffered,*
>
> *1 Corinthians 13:4-5*

Have you ever noticed how important it is when you are with your spouse, for instance, on an anniversary and you go to dinner and there are all these people in the restaurant, but your spouse wants you to treat them like they're the only

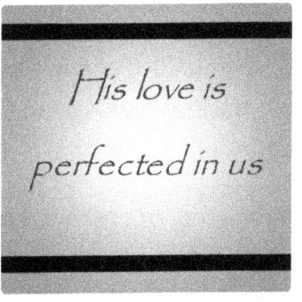

His love is perfected in us

person in the room? Your love makes it seem like no one else exists and they have your full attention.

Have you ever noticed that God interacts with us the same way? He never says: "Can you wait? I have a more important call. Can you get back with me later?" He waits

Condensed Milk

patiently for us, gives us all His attention and loves us like no one else exists. I like that about Him.

I love You, Lord.

The Lord has said one phrase to me more than any other. He has told me this more times than I could count: **I will never leave you or abandon you.** Sometimes He uses the word forsake instead of abandon.

I looked it up, and there are at least 10 verses throughout scripture that express the same sentiment. I was always comforted with the words, but I never really understood them until today.

What this means to me is: He will *never* leave me. He won't say, "I don't love you anymore." He won't ask for a divorce. He won't kick me out, abandon me, give up on me or get tired of me. He plans to stick with me in good times and in bad. In health and in sickness, for richer or poorer, He has my back. Never is a long time in the light of eternity. I can count on Him and trust Him.

Paul wrote of the mystery - Christ in you. Jesus Christ living in you and through you, permanently forever. Understanding this imputes worth and value. Knowing this truth makes me whole, it makes me better, it makes me complete. Does it get any better than this?

His Love

Have you ever wondered why God gives babies to people who have never had children? Isn't the most valuable creation on God's earth a new baby? A new life, a life with potential, a life of new discoveries, new love to enjoy, battles to fight, wars to win, a life of significance, hopefully a life to give back to the One who gave life. Why does God entrust that new life to new parents? Did He do it to help us understand how we should relate to Him? I think so.

> By this the love of God was manifested in us, that God has sent His only begotten Son into the world so that we might live through Him. [10] In this is love, not that we loved God, but that He loved us and sent His Son to be the propitiation for our sins. [11] Beloved, if God so loved us, we also ought to love one another.
>
> 1 John 4:9-11

Look at how great our need is for acceptance - so great that many people follow friends, family and colleagues to Hell. For some people the need for acceptance is so great they will reject God, even when they know the truth.

When I measure myself by others' acceptance or rejection, I will always fall short. As Christians, we need to resist peer pressure and make sure we're gaining our acceptance from God.

Condensed Milk

We have been accepted into the family of God and His acceptance of us should be all we need. We can then walk in the strength of who we are in Him. We can survive the day-to-day pressures of this work and help lead others to Him.

Thank you, Lord, for loving us, for accepting us, just like we are.

30. Why Worship?

I was at church one Sunday. We were about halfway through praise and worship. I was singing but I had also been looking around at all the people there, trying to find my friends, when I noticed a girl worshiping God with her hands stretched into the air and tears running down her face.

I wondered what would cause a person to worship God like that. The Lord had been teaching me about worship. It's easier to praise and worship to music. It's easier to praise and worship in a group. Where two or more are gathered in His name there He will be also.

My understanding of worship started for me a while back when we were attending a charismatic church. There was life there but I struggled with the dancing and the flag-streamer things. I found myself judging people as I looked around in worship so I had to start singing with my eyes closed. That adds a whole level of complexity because I can no longer read the words to the song on the big screen. So I have to concentrate, listen and memorize the words to the songs in order to sing them. I think the best worship songs are the ones where you sing to God, not just about Him.

> *But an hour is coming, and now is, when the true worshipers will worship the Father in spirit and truth; for such people the Father seeks to be His worshipers.*
>
> John 4:23

Well, I found myself singing to God with my eyes closed when all of a sudden I was praying the song to Him. I became aware of His presence and felt like I reached His heart - I really connected with Him. It was a life-changing moment. I grew to love worship. I still do. It's truly revelation from God.

I started leading worship on an acoustic guitar in our small group. I loved contemporary Christian music but I couldn't make myself worship with an electric guitar. I finally figured out what it was. Some of my friends and I had formed a pop band in high school. Don't be impressed; we were horrible. The one bad habit I had picked up though was performing for glory. Once you've experienced that glory - it's like a drug. And it takes more and more each time to satisfy.

Worship is just the opposite. When you worship you are giving glory to God. We are giving glory, honor and praise to our God. If you're not, then your worship is empty.

Why Worship?

Our small group talked me into using the electric guitar to worship. I was playing reluctantly when it was almost like the Lord said let me show what can be done with an electric guitar. I was engulfed in His presence, and He seemed to break the rules of music. I lost the rhythm and started playing beautiful spontaneous worship music - music I'd never heard before nor could I now reproduce.

One day, I asked the Lord, **"Why would you command us to praise and worship You?"** It seemed selfish and inconsistent with what I knew about God. He replied that He commands us to worship Him for our benefit.

We were created to worship Him. There are a great many things that can be said about love. Love is very important. But I suspect we won't ever be complete and satisfied until we learn to worship the Lord in spirit and in truth.

Our group was trying to learn how to be Spirit-led, so we would pray to determine what the Lord wanted us to discuss. I would play the first few lines of each song in my book until I found the ones I felt like God wanted us to sing in worship that evening.

One night I made it all the way through the book but only found two of the three songs I wanted to find. I asked the Lord if He only wanted us to sing two songs. Suddenly the Lord gave me a new song. He just bulk downloaded it into my head. I wrote it down real quick. When the other musician got to our house, he said, "I know this one, and I know this one but I've never heard that one." I told him I had only heard it once. We still laugh about that.

I collect spontaneous worship music. Brian and Jenn Johnson[K], Klaus Kuehn[L] and Kim Walker[M] have recorded some great tracks. Some of this is prophetic worship, God speaking to us with a prophetic word in song, unrehearsed, unplanned and unbelievably nourishing to our soul.

So the next time you're at my church and you look around the congregation, I'm the guy with his hands stretched to heaven and tears running down his face, and I don't care what anyone thinks of me.

31. God Sent Me an Email

It was a beautiful day. I was heading home after work one Friday, in the convertible with the top down, listening to rock music. Not really in a spiritual mode, suddenly the car was full of the presence of the Lord. The Lord said He had a word for a friend at church. Let's say his name was John. The Lord gave me the word (something similar to this):

"Do not fear or be dismayed, the battle belongs to the Lord. Just step back and watch the Lord fight this battle on your behalf. You don't need to do anything."

I told the Lord I hadn't talked to John in a really long time, and I had no idea what was going on in his life. I said, "I can't give a specific word like this without some confirmation. Besides I don't have John's phone number."

The Lord told me to check the group emails from the church for his email address. I moaned, "If this doesn't mean anything to him, he'll think I'm crazy." The Lord asked, "Are you going to trust Me?"

I went home and typed out the email, asked if I got it right and pressed send. What I didn't know was John was in the midst of a very difficult situation. I was aware the Lord

Condensed Milk

didn't want me to know the specifics of his ordeal. By not calling he wouldn't feel obligated to give details.

Unbeknownst to me, John had scheduled a meeting the next morning with one of the pastors to seek advice. The pastors of our church got a kick out of it when he told them, "God sent me an email." Over the next few weeks he stepped back and watched God move on his behalf.

> He still speaks to men

Several weeks later he sent me an email thanking me and said the word was right on.

Later on he sent me another email saying, "You will never know this side of heaven what a difference your faithfulness made in my life." The Lord had done everything He said He would.

This word from the Lord had so impacted John's life that I heard from him again one year later, on the anniversary of the email, and he thanked me once more.

This really underscores the importance of pressing in, waiting, listening and making ourselves available to carry messages for God. Delivering words is not easy and not without risk; however, we cannot underestimate the impact of God in someone's life when we have the courage to step out in faith and share what He has placed in our heart.

Prophetic words

Prophetic words seem to come in several varieties. The three examples I give here are directional, informational and words of confirmation.

The prophetic word for John was **directional**. Typically God won't give you a directional word without it being consistent with what He has already told you. It usually lines up with the Godly counsel that you have already received.

At least in my experience, the Lord has never given me a prophetic word for myself and seldom for my family. Any words for me or my family are more interactive and conversational. Typically the word is for someone who knows you well enough to receive the word or someone you're ministering to.

Over time I've noticed that the words get more specific as we learn to hear Him better. He also gives much more difficult words to deliver, with little or no confirmation. It will really stretch your faith and force you to trust Him.

Alison and I were praying for a woman in our church. Let's call her Jill.

The Lord gave me an **informational word** for her. He told me she had an issue with her father and it was affecting her relationship with Father God. She cried and cried and said she wasn't on speaking terms with her father.

A few weeks later Jill was so happy and told us how she had reconciled with her father and told us of her new relationship with Father God.

Another example, I was sitting in church and the Lord gave me a specific Bible verse and told me to give it to a man I knew there. I didn't know him very well. Let's say his name was Bill. I looked around and couldn't find him. I told the Lord that Bill wasn't there. I doubted that I had even heard the Lord correctly. The Lord said he was there. I looked for him again. We repeated this cycle several times until Bill's wife walked in the door.

I asked her if he was at church that day, and she said he was working in the children's ministry. I found Bill and gave him the verse. He immediately started crying. He sat down on the floor and just cried and cried. When he regained composure Bill told me he had been diagnosed with cancer. The Lord had recently given him that very same verse and told him everything was going to be ok.

It was a **word of confirmation**. By the way, not long after that, God healed the cancer. Isn't God good?

Words of knowledge

Words of knowledge are different from prophetic words. The Lord gives us these to warn us or to tell us something we would have no other way of knowing. I've received words of knowledge for both myself and other people.

Often the Lord will give these words to parents to help them be aware of their children's hidden needs or activities. He may also give you a word at work to help make you aware of something or to obtain a better outcome.

They're not usually something the Lord wants you to repeat. Often the Lord uses this to help explain the behavior or actions of someone close to you.

A good example of a word of knowledge would be the woman at the well (John 4). Jesus told the woman her life story, instantly giving His ministry credibility.

> *For to one is given the word of wisdom through the Spirit, and to another the word of knowledge according to the same Spirit;*
>
> 1 Corinthians 12:8

You don't have to be a prophet to get words from the Lord. When you are praying for somebody, always stop and be quiet and ask the Lord if He has a word for them. And then listen. Often the word He gives you will minister more than anything else you can say or do. There is life changing power when God uses you to speak into someone's life. After all, He spoke this world into existence.

Condensed Milk

When people first start moving in these gifts, it can be stressful. Cut them some slack. Pray in groups, often the Lord will give more than one person the same word. Train yourself to hear better by praying for each other.

Who knows, maybe God will send you an email.

32. Prophetic Dreams

Prophetic dreams, though similar to prophetic words, are more like open visions in your sleep. I've only had a few of these and don't know anyone who has had many. I'm sure someone knows more about this and may have written a book on the subject. My purpose here is to include it in my collection of encounters with God, to help stretch your faith, and so you could know what to expect.

In October of 2001, I had a dream. I knew it was a spiritual dream; I could feel the Lord's presence. The colors were so vibrant, much more real than reality. In the dream, I was on the banks of a large lake or river. It was like a park. There were people playing and picnicking, little kids running. It was a beautiful day outside. The water was still.

I noticed to my left there were four people fishing. They were all fishing with the same kind of pole, same string, all of the bobbers floating the same distance from the shore. **Suddenly as I looked, all the bobbers dipped at the same time, and they each pulled a fish simultaneously onto the shore.**

I stepped up closer and looked at the fish. I'm not much of a fisherman, but that was the weirdest fish I've ever seen.

Condensed Milk

They all looked the same; they were short and fat with a large head, big eyes and a mouth like a gar. Their skin was hard and red like a crustacean. They were very ugly. The first fish looked like a four-pounder. The second was a little larger. The third one was the largest. And the fourth was a little smaller. Then the dream ended.

Things I've noticed about spiritual dreams: I wake up the second it's over with a very clear recollection of the dream. But like prophetic words, if it doesn't originate in your head (in other words God put it there and you didn't think it up), then it has a very short shelf life. You won't be able to remember it very long, so write it down.

Next, I've noticed sometimes He'll give you the interpretation and sometimes He won't. It doesn't hurt to ask. I knew the dream had some symbolic meaning, and I had never seen a fish like that before.

I asked the Lord, "What's the interpretation of this dream?"

He asked me if I had recalled anything like this recorded in the Bible.

"Well, there was that thing about the cows coming out of the Nile River," I said, "but it's not exactly the same" (Gen 41).

He said, "What were the cows symbolic of?"

I guessed, "Years? Then do the fish stand for years?"

He replied, "Yes."

Then I said, "Well, these fish weren't really lean or fat. I would describe them as hard and ugly. Therefore I would describe this time as four hard and ugly years. I would describe the first year as being bad, the second as a little worse, and the third the worst and the fourth a little better."

He said, "That description would work."

I received this dream at the end of the first hard year. It struck me as odd that the Lord would give a New Year's prophetic dream in October as opposed to the end of December or January. I researched and found the first month of the Jewish civil calendar is Tishri that corresponds with September through October. The civil calendar is the official calendar of Kings, childbirth and contracts. Apparently it's the one the King of Kings uses.

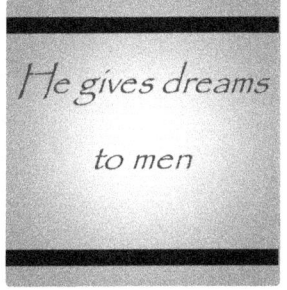

The next question you need to ask the Lord is: What do you want me to do with this? So far He's always given me instructions for whom to give these to. I don't recall ever getting these for myself. He's told me of a few future events, but more as casual conversation.

In this case the Lord instructed me to write down the dream and interpretation and give it to a business owner I knew. As the time passed the Lord accurately predicted with the dream how those four years would unfold.

Once again, I included this as an example of a prophetic dream. This dream has little significance now. Keep in mind there are all kinds of dreams. There are good examples of prophetic dreams in scripture; try Genesis 37 or Daniel 7.

33. Superheroes

Some people want to be heroes. Maybe, deep down, we all do. (I've always wanted to be a superhero.) Some want to be a superhero like Superman or maybe just be heroic without special powers like Indiana Jones. I think some of us want to save the world or maybe just save the day.

Why is that? Do we want our friends or family to be proud of us? Or do we want to please God or make Him proud of us? How do superheroes fit in the Kingdom of God? Is Lex Luthor a type of Satan and Kryptonite a metaphor for sin?

Is it because we are created in the image of God? He saved the day many times and saved the world. And how about those super powers? He heals the sick, raises the dead, walks on water, moves through walls, appears and disappears at will.

What is it about superheroes that catches our imagination?

Are superheroes like God?

Is Jesus the ultimate superhero?

I reflected on how these heroes would use super strength and violence to protect people and dispense justice. I compared superheroes to Jesus. I can't think of any time He used supernatural strength to accomplish anything. I would guess He had access to super strength - clearly an attribute of faith (cast this mountain into the sea) or a capability of angels. He obviously had much more faith than a mustard seed. Jesus did use violence once with the money changers but didn't seem to hurt anyone.

Why does the superhero model look so viable? Samson with his super strength is the closest example to a superhero in the Bible. He did use super strength and violence to dispense justice but it didn't work out so well for Him. **David, with his stand against Goliath, would have made Indiana Jones proud.**

Why didn't Jesus use super strength at all in His ministry? He had more power at His disposal than all the superheroes combined, yet He restrained Himself and chose to live His life as a man. Anything He did supernaturally, He did by the power of the same Holy Spirit who empowers us.

Is wanting to be a superhero a bad trait, just a grab for fame and glory? Maybe it's a result of the fall and a desire to "be god." Do superheroes need people to give them glory and honor? I wonder if it's a need to be in control, to be invulnerable. We might want heroes to keep us safe from harm, but isn't that God's job?

Maybe we just want our God to be more like a superhero. A little more tangible, you know, after all you can see superheroes flying around. They're not invisible like God. They require less faith to believe in, right up to the part where they only exist in our imagination. Still, I love to watch heroes being all heroic at the movies.

Every superhero has a villain. Are there any situations in real life where I could encounter a villain? I thought of someone breaking into our home. I was praying and talking to the Lord, asking His thoughts on using force to protect my family from the villain or in this case the bad guy.

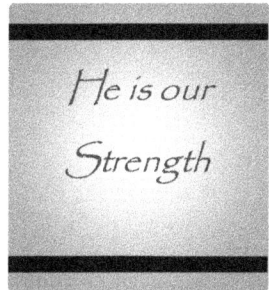

He told me anyone can take a life, but by the power of Holy Spirit you can reach out your hand and give life.

The same power that spoke this world into existence lives in every believer. There isn't anything wrong with a bad guy that can't be fixed.

Hurting people hurt people. Instead of hurting them back, maybe we could partner with God to get their hearts healed.

I included this chapter in the book to make you think. We need to examine our hearts and our minds and our motives in the light of God's Word.

Condensed Milk

We need to contemplate our thoughts and desires and press in to deeper things of God. We need to meditate on God and discover how our reality fits within His reality. We should be careful not to compartmentalize our Christianity from the other areas and interests in our lives. We need to reconcile our world with His so we don't have a part of our life where we involve Him and a part where we exclude Him. We need to let Him into our lives - not just on Sunday. We should be Christians seven days a week.

Have you let Him in? Search your heart and open every room to His light. Give Him your hopes and dreams. Tell Him your hurts. Take Him to school; take Him to work with you. (He's there whether we acknowledge His presence or not.) You can't imagine the potential of this relationship. The King of Kings and Lord of Lords involved in our lives!

Why do I think like I do? Why do I want to be something I'm not? How much of the things you hold to be true really are true? We really don't know how much of what we believe to be true is a lie. We need to seek truth to protect us from error, let Holy Spirit lead us and guide us into all truth.

The greatest Superhero of all, the One who spoke the world into existence, lives in us. He is omnipotent. This means He can do all things; He can do anything. Since Jesus lives in and through me, therefore, I can do all things through Jesus Christ who gives me strength. How much strength is needed to do all things? Is that any less strength than Superman?

The Scripture that follows describes the armor of God. It's kinda like an Iron Man suit.

> *Finally, be strong in the Lord and in the strength of His might. [11] Put on the full armor of God, so that you will be able to stand firm against the schemes of the devil. [12] For our struggle is not against flesh and blood, but against the rulers, against the powers, against the world forces of this darkness, against the spiritual forces of wickedness in the heavenly places. [13] Therefore, take up the full armor of God, so that you will be able to resist in the evil day, and having done everything, to stand firm. [14] Stand firm therefore, having girded your loins with truth, and having put on the breastplate of righteousness, [15] and having shod your feet with the preparation of the gospel of peace; [16] in addition to all, taking up the shield of faith with which you will be able to extinguish all the flaming arrows of the evil one. [17] And take the helmet of salvation, and the sword of the Spirit, which is the word of God.*
>
> *Ephesians 6:10-17*

Please note in this scripture our battle is not against flesh and blood. That's what most superheroes fight.

The significant difference between Jesus and superheroes is the goal of a superhero is to eliminate all pain and

Condensed Milk

suffering. Jesus's goal is to grow us; pain and suffering is a required part of that process. He came not to save us from pain and suffering; He came to save us from death - eternal death.

34. The Mighty Power of God

I had been praying for a family member for about two years. One morning at about 3 a.m., my prayers peaked in frustration. I skated precariously close to the edge of accusation and even judging God. The Lord didn't answer my questions or even address my concerns. Instead He dosed me with what I can only describe as the "Mighty Power of God." I knew I was having a Job Chapter 40 moment. It wasn't what the Lord said. He has been very tolerant of me. It was more one of those eye-opening experiences where the Lord revealed more of who He is and what He's capable of.

I was aware of a very strong presence of the Lord when **He suddenly enveloped me in power** - a transparent layer around me about six inches thick. I could feel it around me, but I couldn't see it. It felt like a thick, soft suit that was awkward to move in. It was also hard to hear anything. I was immediately aware of things I was now able to do. Like I knew I could walk on water. The lake was only out the door and across my neighbor's yard. I thought about walking on the water, but I was wearing my pajamas and it was 3 in the morning. I didn't want to bother my neighbors, and I didn't need to test God. I just wanted to be obedient.

Condensed Milk

I asked, "Lord, what do you want me to do?"

He told me to walk around the house.

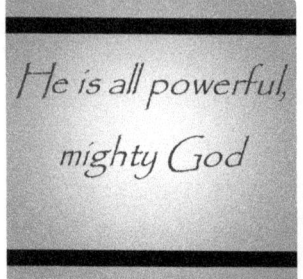

There are a combination of rooms and hallways that connect in a circle on the inside of the house. I knew He wanted me to walk there, so I did. I started to walk around the house; my arms and legs felt so thick. I was aware of how heavy I was. It felt like I weighed over a ton. I was also aware of how strong I was. I was afraid to touch the house; I was afraid I might break it. I completed the first lap and asked the Lord what else He wanted me to do. He said to walk around the house seven times.

So I walked around the house seven times. It was hard to hear anything inside the thick layer of God's presence, but I was aware of the floor groaning. At the end of the last lap everything returned to normal. The Lord ministered to me for a while. He told me everything was going to turn out okay regarding my original prayer concern.

I thought Alison was asleep through all this. When I returned to the bedroom she was awake and frightened. She said she heard me walking around in the house. On about the third trip she heard the foundations of the house shake. On maybe the fifth pass she heard a sonic boom in the distance. Oddly, I didn't hear anything.

The Mighty Power of God

Later, I asked the Lord for an example of this in the Bible. The mighty power of God was at Jericho (Joshua 6) and when Jesus walked on water (Matthew 14). Samson also knew it well (Judges 16). Coincidentally, God had Joshua walk around Jericho seven times.

The Lord didn't address any of my concerns but communicated He is more than capable, all-powerful and mighty.

I need to trust Him more. I need to not underestimate the power of God, and most of all I need to not judge Him when He doesn't do exactly what I want Him to do when I want Him to do it. The better we get to know Him, the more we will trust Him and our faith will grow stronger (Job 38).

We need to keep in mind that the Lord's ministry here on earth was an example for us. He says if we believe in Him then every work He did we can do and even greater things than these.

> *Truly, truly, I say to you, he who believes in Me, the works that I do, he will do also; and greater works than these he will do; because I go to the Father.*
>
> *John 14:12*

We are empowered by the same Holy Spirit that empowered Him. By faith we should be able to walk on water, heal the sick and raise the dead. We shouldn't desire these miracles as a merit badge or for bragging

Condensed Milk

rights, but we need to press in to the Lord and let Him build our faith so we're ready in season when He needs us.

I don't want the Lord to have to bring someone from a distant city to minister because I just don't have the faith to get the job done. We need to be ready. We need to break off those limits we put on ourselves. What part of "I can do all things in Christ Jesus who gives me strength" says except walking on water or raising the dead? No, I've not seen either of these - yet! But I haven't seen a donkey talk either. What I have seen is my God is powerful enough to do what needs to be done.

> *strengthened with all power, according to His glorious might, for the attaining of all steadfastness and patience; joyously*
>
> Colossians 1:11

I want to be part of the solution, not part of the problem. I need to trust God that He can do anything He wants, however He wants and I can trust His judgment. Thank You Lord for teaching us and training us to be more like You.

And the family member I prayed for? Everything did turn out okay. The Lord didn't do anything I asked Him to do. But in a way that only God can, He turned the situation around and blessed almost everyone involved and radically impacted people's lives.

35. Manifestations

"Spiritually, you're now doing what you used to look down your nose at. You're now doing, you are what you used to talk against, and so thankful to the Lord."[N] (This was part of a prophetic word I received.)

What are manifestations? I would define them as physical, demonstrative reactions to spiritual influences.

Some people lump manifestations in with spiritual gifts. They're similar and manifest often at the same time. For example, the anointing makes a huge difference when you're praying for someone. The gifts are predominately for the benefit of other people. The manifestations are more for our benefit like fuel for faith.

> *Now there are varieties of gifts, but the same Spirit. [5] And there are varieties of ministries, and the same Lord. [6] There are varieties of effects, but the same God who works all things in all persons. [7] But to each one is given the manifestation of the Spirit for the common good.*
>
> 1 Corinthians 12:4-7

The first manifestation I was exposed to was the Holy Laughter. As our pastor was speaking, three or four people in different parts of the congregation started laughing out loud. I just wanted them to stop or have someone make them leave. It was so disruptive; I couldn't hear the speaker. He didn't seem to care and was laughing with them and at them (not in the Spirit).

Wow, what a different perspective I have today. Maybe the most significant thing happening in the room that day was Holy Spirit ministering to those people, changing them forever.

Manifestations build faith

The physical touch from God can't be faked. It's not like you can point a fictitious shake generator at someone and make them shake. I looked around and no one was touching me. It could be the Devil was making me shake. But is the Devil more powerful than my God? The Bible says that isn't the case.

And why would the Devil do anything that would also cause me to have an incessant hunger for the Word of God, cause me to pray all the time, desire to be with the Lord and need to worship Him? That would be bad marketing. Why would anyone think I would want to act foolish? I'm so overwhelmed by the love of my Lord - I don't care what people think.

I've looked at these manifestations and studied them. A major component is called anointing. It's invisible; I'm not sure if it exists within the realm of physics. It is slightly thicker than air. It's fluid like a liquid yet it flows more like electricity. It flows easily through people and metal. It can overload your nervous system and make your muscles not work well.

Common manifestations of the anointing are drunkenness and slurred speech. It can also cause twitching, jerking and shaking. If it's on the floor, it puts up a slight resistance when you try to walk through it, like walking in the surf. Most people "under the influence" are happy, silly and/or crying. If a lot of anointing flows into your body, it can be painful at the point of entry for a second. If you push back, Holy Spirit will back off. It seems to be somewhat about relinquishing control, submitting to and trusting the ministry of Holy Spirit.

Christians will often lift their palms toward heaven catching this anointing as if it were falling like rain, filling them with the Spirit and peace. I drive to work with one palm up every day.

Stomach crunches are an interesting manifestation. There's no warning; all of a sudden your stomach muscles contract and push a lot of air out your lungs. If your mouth is open and vocal cords engaged, the result is a loud noise that can be very embarrassing. I have tried, but I can't make my stomach crunch by an act of my own will. Over time I've noticed Holy Spirit often uses this in my life as if to say what you just heard is truth.

We prayed for a paraplegic once and the man's paralyzed leg started twitching. We prayed for an unconscious man in the hospital once and he started twitching while he was still unconscious. John the Baptist jumped in his mother's womb when Mary, pregnant with Jesus, came near him. These would be hard to fake.

> *When Elizabeth heard Mary's greeting, the baby leaped in her womb; and Elizabeth was filled with the Holy Spirit.* [42] *And she cried out with a loud voice and said, "Blessed are you among women, and blessed is the fruit of your womb!*
>
> *Luke 1:41-42*

It's not emotionalism for fun or for show. When you're filled with the Spirit you react sometimes in unusual ways.

Sometimes when you get close to an anointed person it's like bringing two positive magnets together and you can feel it pushing you away from the other person.

Other manifestations include runners, the overwhelming desire to run. (Why, I don't know.) It could be like walking around Jericho.

For me, little manifestations happen from time to time. Significant events where there are large quantities of anointing seem to require a revival or a "move of the Spirit."

Manifestations

Sometimes anointing is warm, like when it's on your hands. The more calm I am when I press into the Spirit, the hotter my right hand gets. The more I pray for people, the hotter it gets. I can measure how much anointing I have by bringing my left palm toward my right. When I feel the anointing on both hands, I look and measure how far my hands are apart. (Right now I'm at about 3 inches. A few minutes ago I was about half an inch).

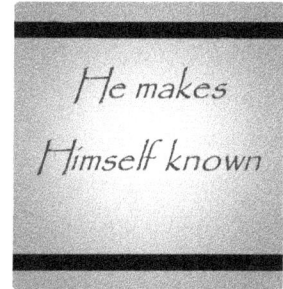

Often when I worship, my right hand will shake, not my left hand for whatever reason. As my daughter was reading this chapter, her right hand started to shake.

Manifestations humble the proud

In high school I used to walk around and slap my hand on people's foreheads and push back and say, "Be healed!"

Later as an adult, I started shaking very noticeably in church one Sunday. Friends and family members were trying to hold me in the chair, quite amused by my behavior.

I asked the Lord why this was happening to me. He referred to the many times I had made fun of Holy Spirit's ministry and said for that I have been blessed with being a fool for Christ. I'm good with that.

Manifestations bear witness

There are those who see the manifestations in others but don't experience anything or feel anything. John Arnott, the Senior Pastor of Catch the Fire Toronto Church, was one of those who had not experienced anything, but believed. Blessed are those who see but don't manifest and still believe. Seeing physical manifestations in others builds faith. When you see it's easier to believe. When a saved person sees a manifestation it encourages them to draw closer to the Lord. When the unsaved see the manifestations it challenges them to have to deal with the reality of God. He's not some ethereal concept but a living God. We need to trust God to do what is best for us in our lives. He will do what He wants in His timing.

Manifestations are a stumbling block

I believe the manifestations are supposed to be a stumbling block. This is a pattern the Lord uses often. He doesn't always package the things of God in ways easy to accept. Like when Jesus said eat my body and drink my blood (John 6:54). Even His disciples could hardly accept it, much less the non-believers.

> *Therefore many of His disciples, when they heard this said, "This is a difficult statement; who can listen to it?"* [61] *But Jesus, conscious that His disciples grumbled at this, said to them, "Does this cause you to stumble?*
>
> *John 6:60-61*

Destroy this temple, and I'll rebuild it in three days (Mark 14:58). You must be born again (John 3:7).

Jesus said these words deliberately, knowing that many people would stumble over them. The people divided into two groups; those who were with Him and those who were against Him. He forced those who were on the fence to choose sides.

If you look at the chapter titles in this book, there's hardly a chapter, the theme of which, someone hasn't stumbled over.

The manifestations are supposed to make us stop and evaluate "Is this of God?" They can't be explained logically. They require faith and trust to believe. How powerful is our God? Is He strong enough to stop any manifestation not of Him? Absolutely. If we struggle with anything, all we have to do is pray and ask Him to help us understand what it is He wants us to know. The Lord still deliberately creates situations where people can choose to stumble. The best plan is to wait or extend grace until we understand what the Lord is teaching us.

The Lord gave me a prophetic word once for three of my close friends. I delivered the word exactly as the Lord gave it to me. I wasn't paying much attention to the content. I was focusing on accurately repeating what I heard. Had they received it as coming from God - it would have blessed their life. But they heard it as coming from me and about me; in that context it sounded very arrogant. They immediately separated themselves from me and have barley spoken to me since.

I asked the Lord why did this happen? Had I done something wrong? He said that no, He gave me the word to separate them from me; they were seeking spiritual gifts with impure motives.

Manifestations divide

Manifestations separate the wheat from the chaff, by the wind of the Spirit. The plagues of Egypt separated everyone into two camps. The ministry of Jesus separated the Jews into two camps.

The move of the Spirit divided our friends. It divided our church. It divided denominations. I saw pastors I loved and respected say, "That's not in the Bible! Holy Spirit won't make you do anything weird." All I know is I was blind (figuratively), and now I see.

Curious point: Of all my secular friends and acquaintances, even atheists I know, I have never been aware of them attacking or saying anything negative about the ministry of Holy Spirit. A few have made jokes about ministers on television. All the angry attacks I have ever seen on the validity of the ministry of the Spirit have come from within the church. Some of my brothers in Christ, the same ones who have taught us not to judge one another and to practice forgiveness, are vehemently opposed to any spiritual manifestations.

Inspect the fruit. A person who manifests is usually desperate for God. We wouldn't yell at and condemn an adulterer in our congregation. Let's reach out in love to those we don't understand.

Manifestations draw people to Jesus

I can remember years ago when we were looking for a church home. I interviewed our friends and found some that "had life." I asked what church they went to. They all were attending one of two churches - a charismatic church and a Messianic church. We visited both. We saw behavior we had never seen in church before, but you couldn't deny they had life. What a change God has made in our whole family. The church took us in, ministered to us, and the Lord drew us to Him.

I don't know about you, but I've had all the dead religion I need for a lifetime. I want to be where there's life. I'm a follower of Christ - I want to go wherever He is. I want to be part of whatever He's doing. I want to rest my head on His heart like the Apostle John. Like Brian and Katie Torwalt, I'm a lover of His presence, and that's all I wanna be.[o]

I have spoken to mature Christians who grew up in a church moving in the ministry of Holy Spirit. They will tell you about the manifestations they've experienced. But they'll tell you they don't experience them very often, if at all anymore. Maybe after being "born again" the manifestations are like when we were little children playing in the rain. As we grow in the Lord, we are less childlike and don't play as much anymore. Maybe I am still a baby Christian because I love to play in the things of the Spirit. Either way, the manifestations have drawn me closer to God.

36. The Dark Side

Let's explore the dark side, if you will. Was Nietzsche right, is God dead?[P] If He's not dead, then does God no longer intervene in the affairs of man? Are we going to say that all manifestations and phenomena not easily explained within the laws of physics are demonic? And is Satan the only one with the power to move beyond physics? Are we to believe that anything supernatural is demonic? **Do we attribute more power to Satan than our God?**

I've heard examples of other religions experiencing the same manifestations we attribute to the work of Holy Spirit. There are also manifestations of the flesh. People have been known to fake it.

I've heard demonic manifestations are sometimes the same or similar. Are all manifestations demonic? Aren't demons spiritual beings too? So does that make all things spiritual demonic?

No! God, man, angels, demons, the Devil and the host of heaven are all spiritual beings. People of all religions - Baptists, Methodists, Catholics, Hindus, Buddhists, even Atheists - are all spiritual beings. You can't make yourself a nonspiritual being by just not believing. Some people are so prideful or naive they cannot accept that they are spiritual. We are spiritual beings created by a very spiritual God. Why should we be amazed if we experience things spiritual?

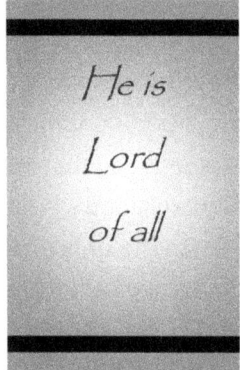

In my research on manifestations, I found that I've observed or experienced many of them. God uses spiritual manifestations to draw us closer to Him and give us something tangible to grow our faith. Doesn't the demonic realm try to copy God? So wouldn't it make sense for the demonic to use things spiritual to deceive their followers?

No wonder, for even Satan disguises himself as an angel of light. [15] Therefore it is not surprising if his servants also disguise themselves as servants of righteousness, whose end will be according to their deeds.

2 Corinthians 11:14-15

When Satan fell, he took a third of the angels with him. It's still two against one before you add the awesome power of God to the mix. I don't think there's that many of them, angels that is. There are billions of people. If there were billions of angels, it seems like we would come in contact with them more.

My opinion only: I suspect the demonic host is not that large. Also, Satan and his demons are hamstringed by the fact that unlike the Lord they aren't omniscient, omnipresent or all-powerful.

I've only come in contact with the demonic a few times. One time I saw the church elders cast a demon out of someone. I was close enough to observe that things demonic "feel dark."

> *Beloved, do not believe every spirit, but test the spirits to see whether they are from God, because many false prophets have gone out into the world. [2] By this you know the Spirit of God: every spirit that confesses that Jesus Christ has come in the flesh is from God; [3] and every spirit that does not confess Jesus is not from God; this is the spirit of the antichrist, of which you have heard that it is coming, and now it is already in the world.*
>
> 1 John 4:1-3

It has been said that the pursuit of the spiritual is the mark of the anti-intellect. I consider myself a reformed intellectual. The Bible says knowledge puffs one up; I've found that to be true in my life. I realized I had more faith in my own intellect than I did in God.

The pursuit of knowing the Lord and understanding the Kingdom of God is man's most noble pursuit.

This is the message we have heard from Him and announce to you, that God is Light, and in Him there is no darkness at all.

1 John 1:5

What I have discovered is that the power of the dark side is insignificant compared to the power of the Lord.

You are from God, little children, and have overcome them; because greater is He who is in you than he who is in the world.

1 John 4:4

37. Raising from the Dead

In 1994 I was listening to Sophal Ung speak (a missionary to Cambodia).^Q He shared his testimony on how they had spent days witnessing in a small village. Only two people were saved.

A few days after they left town the husband of one of the new Christians died. Sophal told how they had a memorial and then placed the dead man in the small house of the grieving widow that evening before moving it the next day to its final resting place. The widow was upset and told the Lord she needed her husband. Not knowing any better she prayed for the Lord to bring him back, and the Lord did!

Interestingly enough, the man woke angry because he was hungry and his wife had not prepared dinner for him. This was similar to when Jesus raised the little girl from the dead (Mark 5:35-43).

At this point I was standing at the back of the church leaning against the wall listening to the story when I realized what it was about.

I said, **"No, Lord! Not the raise from the dead thing.** I can't do the raise from the dead."

I heard my faith thud as it hit the floor. "Don't make me do this. I have believed so much so quickly. Don't make me deal with this, too!"

> *He is not the God of the dead but of the living*

The Lord laughed at me and said, "Look at you. Spiritually I raised you from the dead." Then He gently pinched some skin on my arm and said, "The flesh is easy."

The Lord told me that to raise someone physically from the dead is easy.

To raise someone spiritually from the dead is a process that takes a long time, not to be completed in hours or days but over the course of a lifetime.

> But if the Spirit of Him who raised Jesus from the dead dwells in you, He who raised Christ Jesus from the dead will also give life to your mortal bodies through His Spirit who dwells in you.
>
> *Romans 8:11*

We were born spiritually dead. Even when Jesus raised Lazarus from the dead, he died again later. If we'll believe in Him, the Lord will raise us spiritually from the dead so our spirit will never die.

38. John Chapter 17

One day I asked the Lord, "What do you want me to read today?" I heard Him say John Chapter 17. I read and studied it and found the chapter to be rich and deep. I kept reading and studying it to the point where I would open my Bible and it would fall to John 17. I thought that was because I had spent so much time with it open there. Then I discovered I could open any Bible and often it would fall to John 17.

The Lord is still teaching me out of that passage. It seems I've learned a lot and yet maybe very little; regardless of how much I understand, I'm beginning to grasp the concept of "Inness," of being in Christ Jesus.

> *I in them and You in Me, that they may be perfected in unity, so that the world may know that You sent Me, and loved them, even as You have loved Me.*
>
> John 17:23

This is very important to Him, so much so it was the center topic of a prayer to the Father at the end of the Last Supper. John Chapter 17 is that prayer.

It is my hope and desire that all my brothers and sisters "in Christ Jesus" would come to the realization of what their calling is, and to yield all their being, their will, their plans and desires to the will of God. We need to make sure we're not just playing church and doing good deeds because we 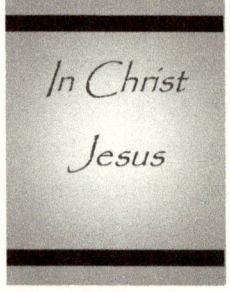 want to. We need to make sure we are seeking the Lord for His will and direction. There are people out there, even serving in the church, doing "good deeds in the name of the Lord" that He never asked them to do nor wants them to do. They're too busy doing their will to do His.

Several times the Lord has told me, **"This is not a game, and we're not playing!"**

> "This is eternal life, that they may know You, the only true God, and Jesus Christ whom You have sent.
>
> John 17:3

The apostle Paul wrote about the "mystery": Christ in you.

> *Of this church I was made a minister according to the stewardship from God bestowed on me for your benefit, so that I might fully carry out the preaching of the word of God, ²⁶ that is, the mystery which has been hidden from the past ages and generations, but has now been manifested to His saints, ²⁷ to whom God willed to make known what is the riches of the glory of this mystery among the Gentiles, which is*

> *Christ in you, the hope of glory.* [28] *We proclaim Him, admonishing every man and teaching every man with all wisdom, so that we may present every man complete in Christ.*
>
> *Colossians 1:25-28*

The Lord is communicating unity, singleness of purpose, the ultimate "let's all get on the same page." If Christ indeed dwells inside us, then He's not very far away. We need to be in unity with Him. We need to set aside our agenda and pick up His agenda, seek His will. Is this not taking up our cross daily?

If we were in unity with God and each other, could not the church, moving forward and operating in love and power that raised Jesus from the dead - the same power that spoke the universe into existence - bring forth the Kingdom of God and change the world?

Wouldn't you want to be part of that?

Condensed Milk

39. Third Heaven

> *I know a man in Christ who fourteen years ago—whether in the body I do not know, or out of the body I do not know, God knows—such a man was caught up to the third heaven.*
>
> 2 Corinthians 12:2

I'm an insomniac. Some of the best times I've had with the Lord are in the middle of the night. Often I'll wake up and look at the digital clock. If the time is on :00 or :30 then usually the Lord wants to talk. On one of those nights I was out in the living room, laying on the couch, with my hands stretched in the air, praising and worshiping God. A pretty normal, uneventful night until all of a sudden I was standing in a very large, well-lit room.

There was a man standing still as a statue 10 or 15 feet in front of me slightly to my left. He was watching someone or something to my right. I was immediately taken back and in awe of the outfit he was wearing. His clothes were amazing, beautiful; they looked expensive like in the $20,000 plus range. The first thing I noticed was his hat. It was a red Fez with a half inch gold band. The gold was so pure it looked translucent.

He wore a robe that was also translucent. You could see into the cloth maybe as much as an inch. It had tiny gold threads woven through the fabric here and there that shimmered in the light (Psalm 45:13). **But the most amazing part was that his clothes glowed, very softly like a dim fluorescent light.** I suspect that he was an angel. Although I can't be sure, it's not like he had wings.

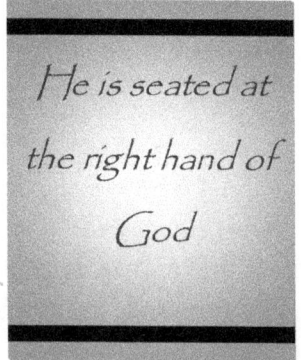
He is seated at the right hand of God

The scene was more like a picture, except every now and then he would glance over at me; he didn't say anything. My senses were overwhelmed; I couldn't seem to take it all in. The person he was looking at came over and knelt down at my feet and started putting something on my feet and shins. It was like a covering, an armor, he was putting on me.

I realized he was talking to me. He stood up and faced me. I was shocked to realize it was Jesus! He continued to talk to me and placed a dull gray cloak over my shoulders. He said it was the cloak of humility. I stood there just staring at Him. It's true what the Bible says, there was nothing remarkable about His appearance. Except His eyes, I was so surprised when I looked at His eyes. I tried to memorize His face. He continued to speak to me. He told me about my future. He told me things too wonderful to hear. I just couldn't bear it.

I would've told you this was a vision except about that time my son's alarm went off in the next room. Every time it beeped, I would get pulled back to the couch for the duration of the beep. When it stopped I would go back across what seemed to be a vast distance and find myself standing again. This repeated several times. I thought it might pull me apart. Then my son turned off the alarm; I found myself back on the couch.

Takeaways: I acted foolishly. I was so mesmerized by the angel, I didn't even notice Jesus. What Jesus said was so wonderful, I couldn't hear it, wouldn't hear it and now I don't know what He said. I do remember it was good.

What He looks like: Most of my energy went toward memorizing His face. But afterwards, His face was erased out of my mind. Seeing His face, I remember I was surprised, but I didn't know why.

Years later, referring to the event, the Lord encouraged me by saying, "Blessed are the pure in heart, for they will see God."

I used to make fun of the brown-haired, blue-eyed pictures of Jesus hanging on the walls of the denominational churches. Don't they know He should look more Jewish with brown eyes?

A couple of years ago, I was spending time with the Lord.

Condensed Milk

He said, "We're not so different you and I."

Immediately I shot back a very sarcastic, "Oh, yeah, we're not so different." I realized how disrespectful my reply had been, and I apologized and sat quietly to see if He would say anything else.

He said again, "We're not so different you and I. Our fathers rejected us because they thought our mothers were unfaithful, but they were not."

I wonder if Joseph struggled with the virgin birth. Maybe Jesus looked significantly different than His brothers and sisters.

My parents divorced when I was very young. My father abandoned me. Later, Mom married a very godly man. I call him Dad.

I met my biological father for the first time when I was 27 years old. I look just like him, more than anyone in his family, only he has brown eyes and mine are blue. Often he told people I wasn't really his child, right in front of me no less. I didn't realize at the time, but discovered later he struggled with my eye color. I Googled it; apparently it's rare for two brown-eyed parents to have a blue-eyed child.

More recently in my quiet time the Lord said, "Before you were born, I snatched you from the fire. While you were in your mother's womb, I changed you. I gave you my eyes."

I said, "That can't be; your eyes aren't blue. They should be brown." He didn't respond.

After much research I discovered that Josephus, secular historian of the period, as well as numerous other ancient scholars and historians, recorded that Jesus's eyes were blue. Who'd a thought?

I've thought about this a lot, and I am guessing that when I saw Jesus what surprised me about Him was His blue eyes. Deep down, subconsciously, I've always known that. It's weird. If you had asked me, I would have told you very convincingly that they were brown, but somehow I knew in my heart His eyes were blue. How or why, I cannot say.

This testimony is so personal I begged the Lord not to include it. The depths to which the Lord interacts in our lives are beyond belief. I might've never known had He not told me.

By changing my eye color, God set in motion events that would culminate in a separation from my birth father. It changed my destiny. My biological father was replaced with a godly, righteous man who loves me, adopted and raised me as his own.

God redeemed me and my family and changed our course for generations to come. Had God not caused these events, it seems unlikely that my family would be pursuing Him now.

I think He does these course corrections to instill confidence in us we'll need later in life. Like when Samuel anointed David to be King when he was still a boy (1 Samuel 16) or when the Lord spoke to Samuel when he was still a child (1 Samuel 3). Another good example would be when Moses was raised by Pharaoh's daughter (Exodus 2).

I suspect the Lord included this chapter so you might examine your own life to see where God has touched your life. Maybe He's changed your destiny. He's more involved in our lives then we can know.

We can't watch a child playing without reaching out to catch them when they fall. God is no different. He can't just watch you without reaching out to help. It's a natural result of an all-powerful Father expressing His great love for us by watching over us all our lives.

> *When he falls, he will not be hurled headlong,*
> *Because the Lord is the One who holds his hand.*
>
> *Psalm 37:24*

We all can have a deeper understanding of who He is. Press in, get to know Him better. Listen for His voice. God still speaks to man.

40. The Hound of Heaven

I struggle with this title. I've heard Jesus referred to as the "Hound of Heaven" in reference to His relentless pursuit of those whom He chooses.[R] I know that everyone doesn't see this side of Him. I did.

How does a guy like me end up being a Christian? Growing up, I learned a lot about God, but I didn't know Him. I went to church until I was sixteen. Somewhere in there I rebelled hard against all authority. I wasn't biased. I rebelled against my parents, teachers, the principal, the police and God. My friends and family would have listed me as least likely to end up in heaven. My childhood friends that have tracked me down recently were clearly disappointed to find out I am now a Christian.

You see, I didn't choose Him, He chose me. I've told Him, "I don't want to have anything to do with You and Your people." I've yelled at Him. I tried to convince myself that this religious stuff was all fabricated by people who couldn't deal with their meaningless existence. I've treated Him very disrespectfully. I told Him, "I don't want to go to your church because I don't want to have anything to do with those hypocrites." **The Lord said, "At least the hypocrites are in a place where they can get help."**

Condensed Milk

The rest of this chapter contains my first four encounters with God. I would call this my testimony. I've tried to be transparent writing this book. I hate lies and I try hard not to lie, even unintentionally. I was that kid in school when the teacher asked who was throwing erasers, I raised my hand.

My first encounter with God was brief but impactful. I was young, it was Halloween and I was alone sitting on the swing in the backyard waiting for it to get dark outside. I was excited about the night, but also very much afraid. I didn't know what happened at the time or who it was, but looking back I know now Holy Spirit came and comforted me. It was as if the air was thicker, heavier. My skin slightly tingled, numb, but it wasn't just a phenomenon of physics. It was like a warm hug; you could feel the love in your heart. It was like the presence of an unseen person, very comforting.

My second encounter with God actually happened in church when I was a teenager. There was a small group of people standing in a circle singing, "There's a sweet, sweet Spirit in this place." I love music and especially good lyrics. They continued to sing, "And I know that it's the presence of the Lord."

I thought to myself, this song is either written by some wishful thinking person, or if true, they've experienced something I don't know. Is it possible all these people are singing this song oblivious to what they're saying? The mindless repeating of lyrics? People sing songs that mean something to them. Is it possible to feel the presence of God? I looked around at their faces. I'm well versed in the scientific method. Happy, peaceful - then I felt that feeling again! I thought that must be real. That would be very hard to fake. I wonder if it's God?

My next encounter with God, I was 17 years old, driving my car around late at night contemplating a new moral sin and strategizing how I was going to make it happen. Today I don't even remember what the sin was.

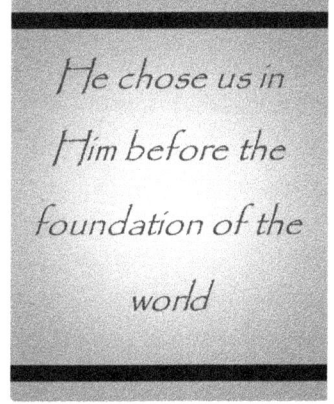

I was in a residential neighborhood driving through a long curve with cars parked on either side of the street. Difficult to maneuver in good circumstances when I heard a voice say, "No! You're not going to do that." My first thought was, "Man, I don't even believe you exist," but I was on the debate team long enough to know denying your opponent's existence was a weak argument. I changed my tack. I said, "I've done this, this, this and this (I named five things I had done); and this isn't even illegal."

He replied that still, you are not going to do this. Go ahead and get this (kind of behavior) out of your system, because after you're married I'm going to draw you back to me.

Condensed Milk

As He was telling me He was going to draw me back, He suddenly went multi-media on me. Rick Joyner calls it an open vision.[5] I could no longer see the road. All I could see was a very high-def picture of me with the Lord's hand reaching for my chest. I thought He was going to grab my shirt near my throat and pick me up off my feet angrily. But when His hand reached my shirt it went transparent, and He grabbed my beating heart and dragged me kicking and screaming toward Him.

That was a pretty accurate prophetic description of what was yet to come. By the way, I didn't commit that particular sin. Nor did I show up at church the next Sunday either. When the vision cleared I had made it all the way around that corner without hitting any parked cars. I don't know why I'm so amazed God can drive a car.

The fourth encounter, I was 19 years old living in a college dorm. I had just met Alison (for the third time) two weeks before. I woke up at 6 a.m. on a Saturday morning. Not many students were awake and with nothing to do I went to take a shower. It was a big shower, not much on privacy, you and your closest 20 friends style shower.

I was alone in the bathroom that day when I heard a voice say, "You're going to marry Alison." That's all He said. He didn't say I highly recommend Alison, or Alison would make a good wife. I knew who it was. I wasn't happy about it either. I thought who does He think He is? God or something? This is not His decision. I will decide who I'm going to marry. I barely knew her.

The Hound of Heaven

One Saturday night not long after we were married, Alison announced she was going to church the next morning. We had a huge fight. I told her if she went to church not to expect me to be there when she got back. But I always was.

Over time she conned me or I lost a bet and we ended up in a Baptist church. The church had a small group that met on Friday nights. I thought that was crazy, sacrilege. They sang worship songs with their hands raised. They would pray for an hour. And they studied The Book of John for an entire year.

These people became like family to us. We grew together and helped each other as our children were born. Our kids grew up with their kids, and God grew our hearts together. And me, I've learned to not kick and scream so much. I'm more of a "Yes, Lord" kind of guy.

As an adult, I read the Hound of the Baskervilles and thought Jesus is just like that hound. He never grows tired, He never gives up. He can be harsh, scary. C.S. Lewis describes Him best, "He's not a tame Lion."

> *So then it does not depend on the man who wills or the man who runs, but on God who has mercy.*
>
> *Romans 9:16*

Why did He pursue me for so long? Why didn't He give up? I have no idea. I've heard a lot of people in my family were praying for me.

Condensed Milk

All the Christians I know heard the gospel and said where do I sign? Not me, I've tried to figure out why I resisted Him so. I think I decided I would rather be an honest sinner than a dishonest Christian and couldn't see how I could ever meet His requirements. Maybe I thought I was a better driver and just wanted to stay in the driver's seat. It probably was that I liked my pet sins and wasn't ready to give them up.

-Thanks, Lord, for not giving up on me. I'm all in now; let's do this!

41. Stranded

A short story. I'm including this because it's so bizarre and yet somehow spiritual. As far as I'm aware all of the people, places and events mentioned in this story are fictitious. I end the book with this.

Enjoy!

Wouldn't you know it, "The vacation nightmare." Car trouble, too late to get it fixed, my wife and I find ourselves stranded in a small town not too far from home but still with no place to stay. We made arrangements for the car and left it parked outside the garage. Nice town, friendly people, they were very helpful.

One of the residents offered, "Hey, we've got this rent house just east of here a couple of blocks. No one's living there right now, you're welcome to it."

It was closing in on dusk as we walked down the quiet street toward the house. We walked through "downtown." Like so many small communities, the downtown area consisted of a long row of run down small stores facing the

Condensed Milk

street; some of them looked vacant, empty. There was a street ministry on the corner, a hangout for local kids, etc. A handful of kids were hanging around the doorway. Everything else was closed for the night.

The house set back off the road about fifty yards, completely hidden by giant evergreen trees. All you could see was a winding sidewalk headed down through the trees. We made our way down past the trees. You can't imagine our surprise ... the house was destroyed!

Leveled, to within one foot from the ground. Ashes everywhere, it had obviously happened a long time ago. Damp, it had rained on it many times. Funny, I noticed there wasn't a single piece of debris larger than a fist. Charred stubs where walls and plumbing had been. How could it have burned up so completely? It looked like it had been about a two thousand square foot home. I was standing in what had been the garage. Odd ... the floor was made of stone. I couldn't tell what kind - just cold gray stone.

I noticed something in the ashes, metallic, golden colored, like pieces of broken jewelry, shattered, as if by an explosion. I picked some up, except where it had been burnt in places, the gold metal was unweathered, untarnished. Hmm, only real gold can do that. It looked like my wedding ring (less the scratches). Oh well, I put the pieces back where I found them, after all they're not mine.

"Come on, Honey, let's get out of here."

You would think the owner knew. How could he not? Practical joke? If so, he sure fooled me. No wonder he was having a hard time renting the place. Oh well, we found another place to stay. The rest of the trip was so uneventful, I can't even recall it.

Years later, we had decided to move out of the city, into one of those cute little towns. Close enough to be near work and yet far enough to be out of the rat race, crime and confusion. My wife had found the ad in the paper: "House For Rent." The house was located in a nice little town, an old town, now reborn. A lot of people had the same idea that we had, and the community was thriving and growing. There were new buildings and new houses everywhere. We found the rent house without much delay. The owners, a nice couple a few years older than us, met us at the door.

"Come in, come on in!"

The house was about fifteen years old, and they had bought it years ago from the original owners. He told me what he did for a living; it was something boring. I don't remember what he said. I asked, "Well, why are you leaving?" She glanced quickly at her husband and said, "We're involved in something new ... we're going to have to move ... we won't be needing the house anymore."

The conversation flowed somewhat nervously until it turned to their belief that: "You can travel through time and space." I looked at my wife, and although I didn't say

Condensed Milk

anything she could see it in my expression, "Loony tunes ... these people are crazy; what have you got me into?"

Crazy, but harmless. Who knows? Maybe this is a chance to witness to them. Maybe that's why we're here.

"Travel through time and space?" I asked.

"Sure," she said, "let me show you." She led me toward the garage while my wife and her husband stayed behind. Dark and gloomy but it looked like any normal garage, and yet ... the floor ... it wasn't concrete. It was stone! Living stone, uncut, this house must have been built on some natural, enormous rock. On closer inspection I noticed a design cut into the face of it. It looked like a big Celtic cross. It covered most of the floor. What could that mean? I bumped into something hanging from the ceiling. There were little gold trinkets hanging by little threads from the ceiling here and there.

I turned to ask her, but she had knelt down on one knee facing the center of the room, the center of the cross. Her charming demeanor had changed suddenly, and she was now very serious, concentrating.

After a moment she said in a soft voice, "Do as I do."

So, I knelt down beside her.

She bowed her head and commanded, "Repeat after me." She paused ... and began to pray, "father of darkness ...."

Terror gripped me. "Noooooooo!!!" I cried as I jumped to my feet and yelled toward heaven, "In the name of JESUS CHRIST!!!"

BOOM! Everything exploded. I staggered through the smoke, "What happened?"

I can't see anything, ashes and debris everywhere. I can't see anyone, no trace of anyone else alive, but yet I don't expect to - after all no one could have survived that. Oh relief, praise God, my wife is O.K. "What happened? Man! Would you look at this mess?" The smoke began to clear, we were alone. The entire house was leveled to within one foot of its foundation. Pieces of metal on the ground.

"Gold?" Déjà vu.

"Whoa ... wait a minute! I've been here before, I saw these very ruins years ago. So I destroyed the house. No ... God destroyed the house."

"Travel through time and space." What a concept—no! What a dream!

I woke up in a cold sweat.

"Stranded" was a dream I had on November 11th, 1989. When I awoke, I went straight to the computer and typed it out. I didn't even understand it until I read it several times. It's been submitted to many people who interpret dreams.

No one has been able to interpret it yet. It's so integrated and complex, I couldn't dream it up (pun intended).

> *"It will come about after this That I will pour out My Spirit on all mankind; And your sons and daughters will prophesy, Your old men will dream dreams, Your young men will see visions.*
>
> *Joel 2:28*

At the core of this dream is the concept of movement through time. Several times the Lord has tried to teach me about His perspective of time and space. He operates in dimensions difficult to grasp. We've had this conversation over and over. Each time He's taught on this subject I've said, "I think I get it." To which He has replied, "You don't get it." I was meditating on this dream and He told me, "You're beginning to get it."

In the dream, look at how He operates within the fabric of time and space. We see the world chronologically. He operates outside of time and sees the beginning from the end and the end from the beginning. He is the Alpha and the Omega, the Beginning and the End.

> *The steps of a man are established by the Lord,*
> *And He delights in his way.*
>
> *Psalm 37:23*

Look in the dream how He caused all things to come together for His purposes. Look back at your life at how He does the same. Look at what He sees and how He sees it. Watch how He intervenes with power. See how He changes what has already happened, how He sets in motion what is to come. See what He sees and what's important to Him.

The Lord is omnipresent; He can be anywhere and is everywhere at one time. But since He operates outside the limits of time and space, He can be at any place in any time at the same time. And we struggle with can we trust Him? Does He see what we're going through? The answer is yes. If we could grasp this, it could change our perspective of how big our God is and what He is capable of.

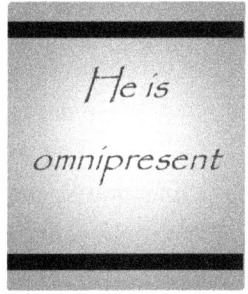

The Lord of the universe loves us and is there with us, for us, when events occur. He's with us in time, across time, all at the same time. He's with us at all the places we are in space, all at the same time. The future isn't a mystery for Him. The future is a fact that He knows and purposes for our benefit, even when we don't trust Him, even when we don't know Him. That's how He knew us when we were in our mother's womb.

How does a prayer today change what He does for us tomorrow? How does a conversation we have with Him ten thousand years from now change what He does for us today? **He just said, "You get it."**

Moving through space

A good example of God's teleporting someone is found in Acts when Holy Spirit "snatched" Philip and deposited him 20 miles away in Azotus or Ashdod. Jesus also teleported.

> *The eunuch answered Philip and said, "Please tell me, of whom does the prophet say this? Of himself or of someone else?"* [35] *Then Philip opened his mouth, and beginning from this Scripture he preached Jesus to him.* [36] *As they went along the road they came to some water; and the eunuch said, "Look! Water! What prevents me from being baptized?"* [37] *And Philip said, "If you believe with all your heart, you may." And he answered and said, "I believe that Jesus Christ is the Son of God."* [38] *And he ordered the chariot to stop; and they both went down into the water, Philip as well as the eunuch, and he baptized him.* [39] *When they came up out of the water, the Spirit of the Lord snatched Philip away; and the eunuch no longer saw him, but went on his way rejoicing.* [40] *But Philip found himself at Azotus, and as he passed through he kept preaching the gospel to all the cities until he came to Caesarea.*
>
> Acts 8:34-40

I was walking down the hall on my way to a meeting. I asked the Lord if He was with me. In a stern tone He replied, "Where you are, I AM. Where you are going, I AM. Where you have been, I AM." I've always seen Him as going wherever I go, but He is already everywhere, both now and across all time.

> *Where can I go from Your Spirit?*
> *Or where can I flee from Your presence?*
> *⁸ If I ascend to heaven, You are there;*
> *If I make my bed in Sheol, behold, You are there.*
> *⁹ If I take the wings of the dawn,*
> *If I dwell in the remotest part of the sea,*
> *¹⁰ Even there Your hand will lead me,*
> *And Your right hand will lay hold of me.*
>
> *Psalm 139:7-10*

If we understand just a little of who He is in time and space, how could we fear anything but Him? How could we not trust Him? He is revealing Himself to us. Do you see how Jesus Christ is our hope?

We, at this point in time, can have hope because He is where we were, He is where we are and He is where we are going. We need to let this soak into our hearts and minds. The fruit of this knowledge and understanding is peace and hope.

> *The fear of the Lord is the beginning of wisdom,*
> *And the knowledge of the Holy One is understanding.*
>
> *Proverbs 9:10*

Condensed Milk

Epilogue

This book may seem like it's all about me, but it's really all about Jesus Christ, for none of this would have happened without Him.

I asked the Lord if this book was ok. It seems so flawed to me. He said He liked it like it was.

I asked Him, "How can You stand our flaws in everything we do when You are so perfect?"

He showed me the outline of a hand drawn with crayon on a white sheet of paper, the art work of my child. Then He showed me a Van Gogh and asked me which one I valued more. I answered the hand. He said He too values His children's work.

May the Lord bless you and keep you and grow you. Don't let pride keep you from sharing what the Lord's teaching you - no matter how bizarre it is. You never know how it will impact another's life. Don't glory in what He's done either - 'cause it's all about Him.

I didn't choose Him; He chose me. I'm so grateful for all He's shown me and taught me. I so desperately want you to know Him even more and experience the fullness of Christ Jesus!

> *'Call to Me and I will answer you, and I will tell you great and mighty things, which you do not know.'*
>
> *Jeremiah 33:3*

If in reading this work you saw love, grace and wisdom, then I was truly successful. That is, I was successful in being transparent enough for you to see through me, to see the One who lives in me, the mystery which was hidden in the past but has been manifested to His church, which is Jesus Christ in you, the hope of glory.

Special Thanks to:

Alison, my beautiful wife. She worked on this almost as much as I did. I couldn't have done this without her.

Christen, my daughter, for her encouragement. She read every chapter as soon as it was written.

Joel Montgomery, my mentor and spiritual father. He has poured so much of his life into me.

David Barron, longtime friend, journalist and author. He really encouraged me to write this and spent so much of his time editing this book.

Kim Deal. She's the book's biggest fan. Her support, love and words of encouragement kept us going.

Margie Knight, longtime friend, editor and author. Her editing and consulting were a great help.

All my friends and family who read the pre-release version of the book. **Tony Nickel, Terry Grimm, Dr. Edward Carew** and everyone else who read parts of the text. Thanks for all the helpful comments.

Mom and Dad. Thanks so much for your support, words of encouragement and great edits.

Condensed Milk

End Notes

A **Benny Hinn** is a noted evangelist, teacher, and the author of best-selling books including *Good Morning, Holy Spirit*. His TV program, *This Is Your Day*, is among the world's most-watched Christian programs, seen daily in 200 countries.
http://www.bennyhinn.org

B **Chuck Swindoll** is an evangelical Christian pastor, author, educator, and radio preacher. He has devoted his life to the accurate, practical teaching and application of God's Word and His grace. A pastor at heart, Chuck has served as senior pastor to congregations in Texas, Massachusetts, and California. He founded Insight for Living, headquartered in Plano, Texas, which airs a radio program of the same name on more than 2,100 stations around the world in 15 languages. He is currently Senior Pastor at Stonebriar Community Church, in Frisco, Texas, and Chancellor of Dallas Theological Seminary. Chuck has contributed more than 70 titles to a worldwide reading audience.
http://www.insight.org/
http://www.stonebriar.org/home/

C **Martin Luther**, 1483-1546. He was a German monk, former Catholic priest, professor of theology and seminal figure of a reform movement in 16th century Christianity, subsequently known as the Protestant Reformation. He disputed the claim that freedom from God's punishment for sin could be purchased with monetary values. He is best known for his work *The Ninety-Five Theses* written in 1517, the disputation protests against clerical abuses, especially the sale of indulgences. Luther taught that

Condensed Milk

salvation and subsequently eternity in heaven is not earned by good deeds but is received only as a free gift of God's grace through faith in Jesus Christ.

[D] **G. K. Chesterton**, 1874-1936. Quote originally attributed to G. K. Chesterton, also found in *Mere Christianity* by C.S. Lewis. Dale Fincher found it to be an alteration of Plato's writings.

[E] **Nan and Bill Bagby**, at the time of this story, were ministering at Sojourn Church. Bill and Nan have been married for over 55 years and are both artists and retired ministers whose ministry experience spans several decades. They came into a personal relationship with Christ during the early 70s and were very involved in the Charismatic Renewal, mainly among the liturgical churches. Their last few years in pastoral ministry were spent mainly training ministry teams together for a variety of churches. After they retired in 1999, they spent nine years in Taos, New Mexico, where they wrote a line of 80 inspirational booklets called the *Seeds of Wisdom Library*. They also published a contemplative journal called *When Quiet Hearts Listen*. In 2008, they relocated their ministry to Paradise, CA.
Author's note: Their ministry had a huge impact on my family. http://www.puremercyministries.com/

[F] **Catch The Fire Toronto Church** of Toronto, Ontario, Canada. Millions of people have come from all over the world to Catch The Fire Toronto (formerly Toronto Airport Christian Fellowship) to be touched and changed by God, returning to their homes on fire for the Kingdom. John and Carol Arnott are the Founding Pastors of Catch the Fire. As international speakers, John and Carol have become known for their ministry on the Father's Love. This Spirit led revival started over 20 years ago.
http://www.ctftoronto.com/

[G] **Bethel Church** of Redding, California. Bethel Church, pastored by Bill & Beni Johnson, has a passion for people, their city and the world. Their culture is characterized by worship, the

End Notes

presence of God, family, revival, miracles, healings, and honor. They have a global impact as a revival resource and equipping center. People from around the world attend Bethel conferences, trainings or their ministry school to experience more of God and the ways of His kingdom.
http://bethelredding.com/home

[H] **Sticking Pennies - YouTube Videos**
http://www.youtube.com/watch?v=fgElvriFhl4
http://www.youtube.com/watch?v=QBKshbHASYY
http://www.youtube.com/watch?v=mSRhlOKKoEM

[I] **Terry Moore** is the Founder and Senior Pastor of Sojourn Church in Carrollton, Texas. He and his wife, Susan, experienced the Holy Spirit in a life-changing way in 1982, and as a result, began a series of home meetings which grew into Sojourn Church. They are motivated by the desire to worship God, share the truth of His Word and minister in the power of the Holy Spirit.
Author's note: A number of events in this book took place during our time at Sojourn Church from 1993-2001. Sojourn introduced us to the ministry of Holy Spirit.
http://www.sojournchurch.org/

[J] **Dr. Charles F. Stanley** is senior pastor of First Baptist Church Atlanta, founder of In Touch Ministries, and a New York Times best-selling author. He demonstrates a keen awareness of people's needs and provides Christ-centered, biblically based principles for everyday life. Today, "In Touch with Dr. Charles Stanley" can be heard around the world via radio and television broadcasts, podcasts, the handheld In Touch Ministries Messenger, and In Touch Apps. His programs are seen and heard around the world on more than 2,600 radio and television outlets in more than 50 languages.
http://www.intouch.org/

[K] **Brian and Jenn Johnson,** Bethel Music. Brian and Jenn Johnson are the worship pastors at Bethel Church in Redding, California. http://www.brianandjennjohnson.com

[L] **Klaus Kuehn,** Klaus Music. Klaus is a worship leader, songwriter and artist for Integrity Music. He is the Director of Pure Worship Ministries and travels extensively releasing worship into the earth.
http://www.klausmusic.com

[M] **Kim Walker-Smith,** Jesus Culture. Kim is a singer, songwriter, worship leader, and recording artist. She is one of the worship leaders for the Jesus Culture band and serves as the Music Label Director and on the Senior Leadership Team.
http://new.jesusculture.com/artists/kim-walker-smith/

[N] Prophetic word delivered to J. David Cummings by **Don Weber.**

[O] **Brian and Katie Torwalt.** Husband-and-wife praise & worship duo Bryan & Katie Torwalt met as worship leaders at Sacramento, California's youth-centered Jesus Culture ministry, where they also served as members of the popular Jesus Culture band. The track, *I'm a Lover of Your Presence,* is from their *Here On Earth* Album from Jesus Culture Music.

[P] **Friedrich Nietzsche,** 1844-1900, was a German philologist, philosopher, cultural critic, poet and composer. He wrote several critical texts on religion, morality, contemporary culture, philosophy and science.

[Q] **Sophal and Deborah Ung** have one of the largest churches in Cambodia. They feed the poor, provide for the needs of widows and minister in refugee camps. They have also built many homes for the homeless and distribute much needed medical supplies. They have seen people miraculously healed, including those who were paralyzed, had long term pain in various parts of their body, excessive bleeding, stomach pain, etc. Sophal and Deborah are

apostles who arrived in Phnom Penh, Cambodia in the early 1990's with a heart to minister to the entire area of Southeast Asia.
http://www.l-c-f.com/missions

R **Francis Thompson**, 1859-1907. Poet famous for the poem Hound of Heaven included in his book *Oxford Book of English Mystical Verse* (1917).

S **Rick Joyner** is Founder and Executive Director of MorningStar Ministries and Heritage International Ministries and is the Senior Pastor at MorningStar Fellowship Church. Rick is President of The Oak Initiative, an interdenominational movement that mobilizes Christians to engage in the great issues of our time. He has authored more than forty books, including *The Final Quest Trilogy*.
http://www.morningstarministries.org/

www.condensedmilkbook.com

www.ingramcontent.com/pod-product-compliance
Lightning Source LLC
Chambersburg PA
CBHW051647040426
42446CB00009B/1023